CONOR McPHERSON

Conor McPherson was born in Dublin in 1971. Plays include *Rum and Vodka* (Fly by Night Theatre Co., Dublin); *The Good Thief* (Dublin Theatre Festival; Stewart Parker Award); *This Lime Tree Bower* (Fly by Night Theatre Co. and Bush Theatre, London; Meyer-Whitworth Award); *St Nicholas* (Bush Theatre and Primary Stages, New York); *The Weir* (Royal Court, London, Duke of York's, West End and Walter Kerr Theatre, New York; Laurence Olivier, Evening Standard, Critics' Circle, George Devine Awards); *Dublin Carol* (Royal Court and Atlantic Theater, New York); *Port Authority* (Ambassadors Theatre, West End, Gate Theatre, Dublin and Atlantic Theater, New York); *Shining City* (Royal Court, Gate Theatre, Dublin and Manhattan Theatre Club, New York; Tony Award nomination for Best Play); *The Seafarer* (National Theatre, London, Abbey Theatre, Dublin and Booth Theater, New York; Laurence Olivier, Evening Standard, Tony Award nominations for Best Play); *The Veil* (National Theatre) and *The Night Alive* (Donmar Warehouse). Theatre adaptations include Daphne du Maurier's *The Birds* (Gate Theatre, Dublin and Guthrie Theater, Minneapolis) and August Strindberg's *The Dance of Death* (Donmar at Trafalgar Studios).

Work for the cinema includes *I Went Down*, *Saltwater*, Samuel Beckett's *Endgame*, *The Actors*, and *The Eclipse*. He also adapted John Banville's *Elegy for April* for the BBC.

Awards for his screenwriting include three Best Screenplay Awards from the Irish Film and Television Academy; Spanish Cinema Writers Circle Best Screenplay Award; the CICAE Award for Best Film Berlin Film festival; Jury Prize San Sebastian Film Festival; and the Méliès d'Argent Award for Best European Film.

Other Titles in this Series

Howard Brenton
55 DAYS
#AIWW: THE ARREST OF AI WEIWEI
ANNE BOLEYN
BERLIN BERTIE
DRAWING THE LINE
FAUST – PARTS ONE & TWO
 after Goethe
IN EXTREMIS
NEVER SO GOOD
PAUL
THE RAGGED TROUSERED
 PHILANTHROPISTS *after* Tressell

Jez Butterworth
JERUSALEM
JEZ BUTTERWORTH PLAYS: ONE
MOJO
THE NIGHT HERON
PARLOUR SONG
THE RIVER
THE WINTERLING

Caryl Churchill
BLUE HEART
CHURCHILL PLAYS: THREE
CHURCHILL: SHORTS
CLOUD NINE
DING DONG THE WICKED
A DREAM PLAY *after* Strindberg
DRUNK ENOUGH TO SAY
 I LOVE YOU?
FAR AWAY
HOTEL
ICECREAM
LIGHT SHINING IN
 BUCKINGHAMSHIRE
LOVE AND INFORMATION
MAD FOREST
A NUMBER
SEVEN JEWISH CHILDREN
THE SKRIKER
THIS IS A CHAIR
THYESTES *after* Seneca
TRAPS

Ariel Dorfman
DEATH AND THE MAIDEN
PURGATORIO
READER
THE RESISTANCE TRILOGY
WIDOWS

David Edgar
ALBERT SPEER
ARTHUR & GEORGE *after* Barnes
CONTINENTAL DIVIDE
EDGAR: SHORTS
IF ONLY
THE MASTER BUILDER *after* Ibsen
PENTECOST
THE PRISONER'S DILEMMA
THE SHAPE OF THE TABLE
TESTING THE ECHO
A TIME TO KEEP
 with Stephanie Dale

Debbie Tucker Green
BORN BAD
DIRTY BUTTERFLY
NUT
RANDOM
STONING MARY
TRADE & GENERATIONS
TRUTH AND RECONCILIATION

Ayub Khan-Din
EAST IS EAST
LAST DANCE AT DUM DUM
NOTES ON FALLING LEAVES
RAFTA, RAFTA...
TO SIR, WITH LOVE
 after E.R. Braithwaite

Liz Lochhead
BLOOD AND ICE
DRACULA *after* Stoker
EDUCATING AGNES ('The School
 for Wives') *after* Molière
GOOD THINGS
LIZ LOCHHEAD: FIVE PLAYS
MARY QUEEN OF SCOTS GOT
 HER HEAD CHOPPED OFF
MEDEA *after* Euripides
MISERYGUTS & TARTUFFE
 after Molière
PERFECT DAYS
THEBANS

Conor McPherson
DUBLIN CAROL
McPHERSON PLAYS: TWO
McPHERSON PLAYS: THREE
PORT AUTHORITY
THE SEAFARER
SHINING CITY
THE VEIL
THE WEIR

Bruce Norris
CLYBOURNE PARK
THE LOW ROAD
THE PAIN AND THE ITCH
PURPLE HEART

Enda Walsh
BEDBOUND & MISTERMAN
DELIRIUM
DISCO PIGS & SUCKING DUBLIN
ENDA WALSH PLAYS: ONE
MISTERMAN
THE NEW ELECTRIC BALLROOM
ONCE
PENELOPE
THE SMALL THINGS
THE WALWORTH FARCE

Steve Waters
THE CONTINGENCY PLAN
FAST LABOUR
IGNORANCE/JAHILIYYAH
LITTLE PLATOONS
THE UNTHINKABLE
WORLD MUSIC

Conor McPherson

PLAYS: ONE

Rum and Vodka
The Good Thief
This Lime Tree Bower
St Nicholas

with a Foreword and Afterword by the Author

NICK HERN BOOKS
London
www.nickhernbooks.co.uk

A Nick Hern Book

McPherson Plays: One first published in Great Britain in 2011 as a paperback original by Nick Hern Books Limited, The Glasshouse, 49a Goldhawk Road, London W12 8QP

Reprinted 2014

This collection originally published as *McPherson: Four Plays* in 1999.

This collection copyright © 1999, 2011 Conor McPherson

This Lime Tree Bower copyright © 1996 Conor McPherson
Rum and Vodka copyright 1996 Conor McPherson
The Good Thief copyright 1996 Conor McPherson
St Nicholas copyright © 1997 Conor McPherson

Foreword copyright © 2011 Conor McPherson
Afterword copyright © 1999 Conor McPherson

Conor McPherson has asserted his right to be identified as author of this work

Cover image by Conor McPherson
Cover designed by Ned Hoste, 2H

Typeset by Country Setting, Kingsdown, Kent CT14 8ES
Printed in Great Britain by Mimeo Ltd, St Ives, Cambs, PE27 3LE

ISBN 978 1 84842 221 6

CAUTION All rights whatsoever in these plays are strictly reserved. Requests to reproduce the texts in whole or in part should be addressed to the publisher.

Amateur Performing Rights Applications for performance, including readings and excerpts, by amateurs in the English language throughout the world should be addressed to the Performing Rights Manager, Nick Hern Books, The Glasshouse, 49a Goldhawk Road, London W12 8QP, *tel* +44 (0)20 8749 4953, *e-mail* info@nickhernbooks.co.uk, except as follows:

Australia: Dominie Drama, 8 Cross Street, Brookvale 2100, *fax* (2) 9938 8695, *e-mail* drama@dominie.com.au

New Zealand: Play Bureau, PO Box 9013, St Clair, Dunedin 9047, *tel* (3) 455 9959, *e-mail* play.bureau.nz@xtra.co.nz

South Africa: DALRO (pty) Ltd, PO Box 31627, 2017 Braamfontein, *tel* (11) 712 8000, *fax* (11) 403 9094, *e-mail* theatricals@dalro.co.za

United States of America and Canada: Curtis Brown Ltd, see details below.

Professional Performing Rights Application for performance by professionals in any medium and in any language throughout the world should be addressed to Curtis Brown Ltd, Haymarket House, 28-29 Haymarket, London SW1Y 4SP, *tel* +44 (0)20 7393 4400, *fax* +44 (0)20 7393 4401, *e-mail* cb@curtisbrown.co.uk

No performance of any kind may be given unless a licence has been obtained. Applications should be made before rehearsals begin. Publication of these plays does not necessarily indicate their availability for amateur performance.

Contents

Foreword	1
RUM AND VODKA	7
THE GOOD THIEF	49
THIS LIME TREE BOWER	85
ST NICHOLAS	135
Afterword	179

Foreword

I was watching a TV programme the other night, the thesis of which was that Irish playwrights failed the Irish people during what was known as the Celtic Tiger period (roughly 1995–2007), when unprecedented prosperity raged through Ireland. The presenter of the show suggested that while Irish theatre had a duty to warn audiences that our fleeting prosperity was about to lead us to doom, in fact plays from this period tended to avoid political issues entirely. Given that I was extremely active as a playwright during these years I have to throw my hands up and say in one sense I'm guilty as charged because I've never written a play ostensibly about economics or politics. Suffice to say this TV programme got me thinking about what politics in the theatre really means, and what it means for the plays in this volume.

It's twenty years since *Rum and Vodka* was written and performed. I was twenty years old when we did it. In Ireland at that time emigration was rampant. The eighties had seen huge unemployment and a kind of drabness pervaded everything.

However, I remember there was a feeling in the air that the nineties could be a time for positive change. Mary Robinson had just been elected as our first female president. After the Irish soccer team had reached the quarter finals of the World Cup, anything felt possible.

By the mid-nineties as borders melted away in the European Union, money and trade began to flow our way. There was a confidence none of us could remember feeling before. Coincidently, in my own field, a wave of young playwrights was flooding theatres in London, New York and beyond. Our work was being translated into many languages. It seemed as though the world was suddenly interested in what it meant to be Irish. We represented a place where a horrendous past met a glistening future and where tradition evolved.

The old monolithic enemies of change seemed to wither. Contraception was finally available in the shops. Divorce was no longer considered a fate worse than death. Single-party government was no longer possible because it just wasn't cool any more. Young Irish people were tired of what Irish 'politics' had meant for so long. For us it was a term tangled up in the violence and sectarianism of our past but finally, thankfully, that all seemed to be winding down with the signing of the Good Friday Agreement.

The emergence of the Progressive Democrats, a party committed to low taxation and small government, had a massive influence. The new key to prosperity was 'light-touch regulation', i.e. banks and businesses needed space to prevail so governments should butt out, keep taxes low and ensure credit was unfettered. Once this idea caught hold in Ireland, a country so accustomed to poverty, it seemed like the money tap would never be turned off. Books were written about our rapid economic transformation and we were held up as an example to developing countries all over the world.

But then something darker happened, perhaps around the turn of the millennium. The insecurity at the heart of the Irish psyche reared its wild sleepy head and roared 'Surely to Jaysus this can't last!' And it no longer seemed to be enough to have a job and support your family; now it felt important to shore up one's nominal wealth in order *never to be poor again.* One must remember that just four or five generations previously, Ireland had experienced a catastrophic famine which altered Irish society indelibly. Deep in the Irish heart lay this almost unspoken, and truly haunting, worst-case scenario. Owning property was a blanket which kept away the bite of fear. No matter how good things seemed to be, many of the burgeoning Irish middle class were compelled to attain what they had never had before; a family house, a holiday home, and a couple of apartments to rent out as an investment. Usually each of these was obtained by securing a mortgage on the other in a draughty house of cards.

All these mortgages didn't seem like a problem at the time because property prices just kept rising. As soon as you'd bought a property you had made money on it, so European banks were happy to lend to Irish banks who were desperate to lend to Irish people. So a construction rampage ensued. By the mid-2000s developers were building apartment blocks for foreign workers to come and live in while they built apartment blocks for foreign workers to come and live in while they… and bang, in September 2008 the credit crunch arrived. The cheap foreign money disappeared. It was payback time and we couldn't pay.

Our economy promptly collapsed, our banks all went bust, and the whole desperate, delusional frenzy ended in a mountain of personal debt. The state stepped in to guarantee the entire country's borrowing responsibilities but it was a disastrous bluff. We

staggered on for a while but before long we ended up in the arms of
the International Monetary Fund, powerless and back where we'd
started in 1990. In fact it was worse, because now unemployment
and emigration had returned *and* we owed everybody a fortune.

A litany of blame blazed across our radio airwaves for months on
end. Everyone suddenly had something to say. Whereas during the
Celtic Tiger nothing seemed political – only economic – now
everything was political. Horrifyingly, even a group of newspaper
columnists and sports commentators banded together to declare
their political intentions. However, when they suddenly backed
down we realised that only professional politicians truly wanted the
impossible job, because it was the only job they had.

So there I was the other night, watching this TV programme about
how Irish playwrights apparently failed to write about all this stuff,
but over the next few days I began to wonder if the programme was
actually missing the point of what art does and how time reveals it.
I had a look back over the successful plays from the time and
speculated if (like looking at the rings in a fallen tree) it's possible
to argue that our theatre history contains the unmistakable mark of
its climate at this time.

The nineties in Irish theatre will probably always be associated
with the monologue. Almost every successful new play that
emerged from Ireland at the time had an element of direct
storytelling. It was as though the crazy explosion of money and
stress was happening too close to us, too fast for us, making it
impossible for the mood of the nation to be objectively dramatised
in a traditional sense. It could only be expressed in the most
subjective way possible because when everything you know is
changing, the subjective experience is the only experience. For
example, a seemingly modest play like *Eden* by Eugene O'Brien –
which consisted of a married couple speaking directly to the
audience for two hours in the Abbey Theatre's studio space –
became a smash hit. It was revived, toured and transferred to the
bigger Abbey space, returning again and again over a period of
about two years. It even made it to the West End (where admittedly
the British critics scratched their heads and wondered at its native
popularity).

I would suggest that the hunger for this kind of highly personal
work was unprecedented because the whole phenomenon of living
in Ireland at the time was unprecedented. It has been argued
elsewhere that a secular need flooded the space left by the
disgraced Catholic Church and a contemporary dearth of true

political leadership. We still had souls, but we just couldn't trust anyone with them any more. Thus monologue theatre flourished because it was a mirror which took you inside your own eye. The work had to become more private and the humour more painful in order to reflect the mood of an audience who didn't feel like they were living in a sustainable reality on any level. Big old 'state of the nation' plays simply couldn't have reflected that feeling, I don't think. The dramatic problem was far subtler than before so the successful plays of the time took a subtler approach.

As young writers, we knew of Beckett's great monologue plays and Brian Friel's iconic *Faith Healer*, but these were examples of a form rather than the norm. When one considers the tumultuous time in which this form re-emerged and became almost ubiquitous it doesn't feel like mere coincidence, and I would contend that to dismiss such a sea change in Irish drama is to ignore how well it charted the peculiar history of the Irish mind for its time. And all the more so when one considers how organic and unconscious this movement was. It just happened. The more Ireland's economic fortunes appeared to catapult us into a twenty-first-century orbit, the more our theatre seemed determined to return us to an almost ancient mode of storytelling.

For myself, I haven't written a monologue play for well over a decade now. This year I am forty and consider myself extraordinarily fortunate to have worked as a playwright for the last twenty years. The hard-won perspective of the intervening time shows me that I thought I was free and independent back then, but now I know I was struggling with history just like everybody else. I used to find it so difficult to even think about my own past work. I always felt the need to look away into the future. But as I enter middle age I look back with a more forgiving regard. I read the very first line of the first play in this volume, which says: 'I think my overall fucked-upness is my impatience.' It was true then, and it's true now, and probably not just for me. And maybe that impatience drew me to the monologue form. Because it could take you right where you wanted to be so fast and keep you there because it just felt real.

At every performance the audience suspend their disbelief. They know they are watching people pretending yet they believe they are seeing something real and true. This is the magic of theatre, and it's purer than film because the audience generate this belief without any of the aids of cinema. A bare story told by a single voice in the theatre can distil this experience even further. Of course it takes a good story and a good actor to tell it. And of course it's probably not for everybody, but for those who like theatre for precisely what it can do best, i.e. create a world out of nothing, this kind of work can be surprisingly memorable.

That said, I want to reiterate that all of the work in this volume is unconscious. I was between the ages of twenty and twenty-four writing it. I knew little about myself and less about the world. I had no insight, political or otherwise. And now? Well, I probably still have the impatience, but regrettably, like all of us who've lived through the last twenty years, so much less of the innocence.

Anyway, welcome to the past.

Conor McPherson
Dublin, August 2011

RUM AND VODKA

For The Fly by Nights

Rum and Vodka was first performed at University College Dublin on 27 November 1992.

Performer Stephen Walshe
Director Conor McPherson

It was subsequently performed by Fly by Night Theatre Company at the City Arts Centre, Dublin, on 30 August 1994.

Performer Jason Byrne
Director Colin O'Connor

Part One

I think my overall fucked-upness is my impatience.

I could never wait for anything to be over.

And I think that's the sign of an inquiring mind.

I don't want to do the investigations, I just want the answers.

And I reckon that because of that I'm a bit of a pessimist.

Because I never got any.

And that can lead to a lack of social graces.

I always feel that wherever I go, people look at me with a squinty face as if to say 'Now, just who the fuck are you?'

I think I hate the human race.

And I think they know it.

I often think the world gets together behind my back while I'm on the jacks or in bed and makes hasty decisions about new ways to get me to leave the planet.

They leave the meeting laughing.

Now, that's got to be the king of conspiracy theories.

But I know it's not true.

I suppose my impatience is due to my embarrassment a lot.

Maybe I don't like myself too much.

I hate looking back at things I've done.

So I'm always doing something new.

That means that my memories are like being different people.

But that's all a load of shit.

What I really want to tell you about is what's happened to me over the last three days.

I'm twenty-four going twenty-five.

I live on a new, well fairly new, estate in Raheny.

I'm married.

I have two young girls.

Until a couple of days ago I worked for the voting registration department of the corporation on Wellington Quay.

I'd been working there since I got married.

When I was twenty.

You might think that's quite young for someone to get married these days.

And I probably agree with you.

But em . . .

I had been going out with a girl since I was eighteen. We had been going out for two years.

And I mean, you're twenty.

What the fuck do you know? I mean, I was still trying the world for size.

Do you understand me? I was arsing about.

You know? I was messing.

With other girls.

I don't think I ever meant it to happen.

It usually happened when I had too much to drink.

But, ah . . . I was at this party one night and I ended up half-comatose in the back garden.

And this girl, friend of a friend, decided she was going to look after me.

While I got sick in her shoe.

She stayed with me all night.

And I was grateful and I thought I felt something for her, and as the night wore on and everyone went home it was mostly horny.

I'm not going into the sordid details.

My life's one big sordid detail.

But we ended up being intimate.

On a number of occasions that night.

And I ended up seeing her for, well, whatever reasons after that.

And all the while I was still going out with my girlfriend and this other girl, the party girl, knew I was. Alright?

And then when the chewing gum lost its taste I stopped seeing her and decided to be faithful again.

For, well, forever.

But then I got a phone call from the party girl.

She was having a baby.

And now she's my wife.

You have to understand I didn't marry her for religious or moral . . . I mean, we didn't have to get married at all.

But as more and more people found out . . .

My mum and dad were furious.

My friends thought I was a fucking fool because they liked my girlfriend.

And my girlfriend.

Well I think it's the worst thing that ever happened to her in her life.

And . . . I have nothing else to say about that except that sometimes I . . . miss her.

So anyway.

There I was.

Lowest of the low, with no one really to turn to except this pregnant girl.

And she was the only one who didn't criticise me.

We got on well enough and the more shit I got off other people the more I found comfort with her.

I ended up saying, 'Fuck you, everybody!'

Got a job, hundred and eighty quid a week, got a mortgage and figured my life finally had some direction.

And I got down to it.

I was the real nine-to-five animal.

And it was alright.

I spent the next two years getting on with making money, getting my wife pregnant again and drinking at the weekends.

The thrill of having your own house.

I could do what I liked.

I was a pretty good family man.

I remembered birthdays and I was Santa.

And the freedom.

I was always waiting for a knock at the door and a slap. But it wasn't going to come. I was grown up. I was allowed.

If I wanted to I could drink till three o'clock, watch videos till dawn, fuck my missus.

I mean, she was always there.

And that's one thing about that marriage.

Maybe there's never been too much . . . I don't know, but that's always been more than made up for in the bedroom.

Even from the outset.

We were married in a registry office.

There was very little ceremony.

But we spent our honeymoon in the house we were buying.

In Raheny.

And even though she was quite pregnant we got up to some of the weirdest stuff.

She's always been insatiable.

She often wakes me up with a cup of coffee which is like just an excuse.

She wants me there and then.

Even when she was huge with the baby she'd insist on doing it standing up with me behind her.

The complaints department weren't exactly run off their feet.

The kids came in a year of each other so we really had two babies in the house for a while.

I've never been gone on kids but I got a real kick out of these girls.

I know it's cruel, but I used to laugh at them trying to walk, falling on their arses or walking into chairs.

I thought that was very funny.

But as they got older I sort of felt like I was just playing at being Mr Daddy.

And it all got a bit unreal. A bit hard to believe.

I still felt eighteen or sixteen.

And it came as quite a shock when I realised that this was as good as things were going to get.

I found myself ticking off the minutes at work, skiving in and out of flexi-time, and, most importantly, drinking a lot.

This year especially it's got to the stage where I'm getting pissed every day.

The only days I don't drink are the ones where I'm too sick to move.

And it's this that really leads me on to the last three days.

Maria, my wife, and I've been fighting a lot recently.

She's been giving out about the money I'm spending, saving nothing, not coming in till one or two every morning.

Thing is, on top of everything, I'm an awful stupid bastard with money.

I don't drive and I jump in and out of taxis like there's no tomorrow.

I know it's ridiculous, but I don't know . . .

I'm just lazy . . .

I'm a thick fucker.

I tried cycling into work for a while.

I haven't cycled in years and Maria said it would keep me in shape as well as cutting down on expenses.

It worked for about three days.

I left the bike in the car park under work, but that meant it got locked in after six.

If I wanted to go for a few jars I'd have to lock it on the street somewhere.

I locked it to the railings of a house on Wellington Quay but then I decided to lock it inside the railings to make it harder to nick.

It worked because it was still there at half twelve that night.

Trouble was . . . my judgement was impaired.

When I unlocked it it fell right down into the basement.

All the lights in the house went on.

I ran down Wellington Quay because sometimes I'm shy.

I had no money for a taxi and I started walking, thinking I'd get the bike back in the morning.

I must have gotten some fright though, because only when I was half way up North Strand did I realise I was holding half a U-lock.

I think I'd have to say that my drinking or habitual drinking is due to two of the men I work with.

Phil Comesky and Declan Short.

They live together in a house in Killester which is the most disgraceful kip I've ever seen.

There's leftovers and remains of about a thousand takeaways, bottles, cans, socks, the place stinks.

It's a mixture of rotting and deodorant. They must spray the air.

I've ended up there hundreds of nights.

They drink, I mean drink, get drunk every day. They smoke about forty each as well.

They're both odd in their own ways.

Declan's got this girlfriend he's been going out with for about ten years.

They always fight. But you should see her drink. Pints. That's what keeps their flame aglow.

They fall around in each others' arms at closing time. Then they get two naggins. Vodka for him, Jameson or Powers for her, as long as it's Irish.

Every day. I'm serious.

Declan doesn't even have a beer belly.

He's one of those people who can drink a keg of Guinness, get four hours' sleep, and still look like he runs a health-food shop.

I sometimes think that he'll be eating his breakfast one morning and it'll catch up with him. He'll disintegrate in seconds.

His girlfriend is a state though.

She looks like her mother shat her.

And that's pure drink.

Phil's the real spacer though.

He's been in and out of mental homes up till a few years ago.

When he was fourteen a boy on his road was killed when he was hit by a car.

It was a big tragedy at the time.

Big turnout at the funeral.

The boy who'd been killed had a girlfriend. They had been going out for about three weeks.

I mean. At that age.

She threw a letter into the grave when the coffin was being lowered.

And . . . she was young. She got over it.

She grew up.

Now, when Phil was twenty, no one knows why, because he didn't even know the girl, he dug up the grave and got this letter out.

He broke into the girl's house at three o' clock in the morning, sat on her bed, and read it to her.

Nearly drove her mad.

I mean. That's real bonkers for you.

Anyway.

Last Friday lunchtime we were out having a drink.

We sank four pints each and I knew the weekend was going to be bananas.

I had been so depressed all week that to get paid meant get pissed.

Trouble was I was already hungover from the night before and my body was staging a coup.

I was finding it difficult to keep anything down.

All I wanted was to put my head on the desk and die.

I would have knocked off early saying I was sick, but there was some fuck-up with the cheques and no one was getting paid till four.

So I sat there sleepy and sick.

Bored stupid, wondering how I was going to get through the afternoon.

And everything went haywire.

Even now it's a blur.

Eamon Meaney, our arsehead of an office manager, came over to my desk in his Farah slacks and Clarke's shoes.

He used to be a national school teacher but he threw a tantrum one day and got fired. He was completely bald and thought he was gorgeous.

He had two queries with my work, and while I tried to dig myself out of a hole full of shit, I saw his expression change.

'Have you been drinking?' he asked me.

'I had a glass of wine with my lunch,' I slurred.

I must have smelled like a brewery, because he asked me just who I thought I was, getting drunk on tax payers' time and money.

I said I didn't know.

He told me to get into his office and walked off.

And I sat there.

Looking at the buildings on Batchelor's Walk, all falling down and filthy.

I saw the last name I had typed on my Apple Mac, Helen Falconer.

What a name.

Her ancestors must have been falconers.

Wow, I thought.

Meaney shouted across the room at me to hurry up.

Everyone looked at me.

People from every county.

I went red from my shoulders to my scalp and . . . I picked up my terminal, and I swung it out the window.

It sailed down two flights and right though the windscreen, and I didn't mean this, of Eamon Meaney's car.

Okay, I had a choice.

I could pretend to have a nervous breakdown and beg everyone's pity, or I could brazen it out.

'Do you have any idea how long I've wanted to do that for?' I said.

They stared at me.

Meaney took a step backwards.

I picked up my jacket and strode out of the office.

As I went down the stairs I heard the door slam. I hadn't meant it but I was glad it did.

The day was overcast and people moved about on the street.

I went straight to The Norseman.

A pint and a short.

Never drank so fast.

Same again.

People in the pub.

Friday lunchtimers taking the afternoon off. Justified. They'd done their work.

And I felt so stupid and sick and guilty and angry and . . . low.

I wasn't very happy.

But I was glad of a drink.

It took the edge off my worries.

Brought out my self-reliance.

If things are going well it helps you congratulate yourself.

If you're in the shitter it gives you all the righteous indignation of an innocent victim.

And by five o'clock I felt both.

At six Phil and Declan came in.

I was quite a sensation.

By seven we were discussing my future plans.

Fuck, the three of us'd go into business together.

We were going to be gardeners.

Out in nature and stuff.

No more fluorescent lights or instant coffee.

And oh yeah, no more drinking.

It was time to take our lives by the scruff said Phil and he got change for the cigarette machine.

We were mates said Declan.

I told the lads I loved them.

I told them I'd wanted to say that for a long time.

We all embraced and I went for a piss.

By ten the place was jammed.

None of us were talking much.

Just drinking.

I thought I was getting a temperature.

The floor swayed and I puked on the carpet.

We moved away from that spot and since the barmen hadn't seen, we got another one in.

By eleven I was nearly asleep.

The whole day felt like something that had happened to someone else.

I put my head in my hands and cried.

I cried until my eyes stung, till my gums felt swollen, till I couldn't lick my lips.

Then it was time to go.

Phil and Declan were arguing about economics. The argument went something like 'Fuck you.' 'No fuck you.' 'That's bollocks.' 'You're a cunt.' 'Me?'

Like that. Like every fucking night.

Declan bought a bottle from behind the bar and we headed for the lads' house.

We had to stop the taxi for me to be sick and while I did, Phil ran up the road and got a Chinese.

Declan's girlfriend was back at the house with some friend of hers from Denmark.

I tried some whiskey but my throat was raw and I nearly got sick again.

Phil vanished upstairs with Miss Denmark and Declan and Siobhan crashed out on the couch.

I went outside. It was nearly two.

I walked along the Howth road to Raheny.

I turned left up Station Road and into my estate.

We live in at the back, in a cul-de-sac.

I went in quietly and took four paracetamol.

The lights were all out upstairs.

I undressed in the dark.

I was too tired to look for pyjamas.

I just slipped under the quilt and stayed as far over my side as possible.

I curled in a ball and shivered.

Maria moved close and held me.

I knew I was going to break her heart.

I'd always known it.

I wished I could wake her up and talk but I was too tired to think.

And then the curse of any tender moment, an erection.

I suddenly wanted her more than ever.

And drink'll do that to you.

And all this . . . aggression.

This is my house.

I'm in bed with my wife.

And I'm going to fuck her now.

I rolled over and felt her tits.

She was warm and soft.

I pulled the front of her nightie up and felt between her legs.

She was fast asleep.

I waited till she was ready, then I held myself above her like I was going to do press-ups, and I slid inside her.

Suddenly it was bright.

It was morning.

The kids were shouting out the back.

I had a massive headache.

Like something was bursting out of my head.

My throat was sore and my mouth was so dry my tongue grated along the roof of my mouth when I unstuck it from my teeth.

And then I remembered . . .

Everything came flooding back and my stomach leapt.

This was very serious.

I could go to jail.

I needed a drink.

Fuck. Had I pulled out of Maria? Had she woken up to find me stuck up her? Did she have to push me off with disgust? I could hear her in the kitchen.

What was I going to say? I wanted to crawl under the quilt and hide like a kid.

I got up.

My clothes stank of smoke.

I put on Maria's dressing gown and went down to the kitchen.

'Hi, hi.'

'You were late'

' . . . Yeah.'

She didn't seem any more annoyed than usual.

I must have pulled out.

I mean, that's pretty close to rape.

She'd have done her nut.

The kids saw me. 'Daddy, Daddy.'

I didn't know which was worse my headache or my guilt.

I couldn't take any tablets because Maria would start on at me about drinking.

I didn't want that.

What I was really worried about was how I was going to tell her I didn't think I had a job any more.

I ate a greasy fried egg I knew wasn't going to stay down, went upstairs, turned on the shower and puked into the toilet.

The shower was cold.

The immersion hadn't been on and I couldn't get a lather from the soap.

You see, this was a bit of a crisis because every Saturday we do the big shop.

We go down to Crazy Prices in Kilbarrack.

I knew I had about twenty-five quid in my jacket, but the messages usually come to about forty-five/fifty.

I was in trouble.

There was no way of not facing the music.

I had to tell her I'd no cheque.

But she was busy when I got dressed.

Getting the buggy ready, I don't know.

I was so tired.

I sat in the living room and closed my eyes.

I had no idea how to go about this.

Then we were up and out.

Walking down the street.

Carol in my arms.

Niamh in the buggy.

Maria saying hello to people.

Up Raheny Hill.

Carol's hair on my face.

Into the car park.

It was starting to drizzle.

We got a trolley, Maria's list, and we were shopping.

I was forming mad plans.

I'm on a diet, I don't need food.

Let's have a severe economy drive.

But she'd know something was up.

And it was.

Something was up.

The trolley was filling up.

Maria was saying, 'Pampers, Pampers, toilet roll.'

I was pushing the trolley.

'Maria . . . '

'Yogurt, cheese . . . '

'Maria . . . '

'Mm?'

'Maria, I just remembered.

I never cashed the cheque, we got them late and I . . . '

'What . . . ?'

'I think I've lost my job.'

'What are you saying? Put that down Carol.'

'I threw my terminal out the window.

I'm so sorry.'

Maria went white.

She was puzzled.

She wanted this to be a joke but she knew it wasn't. And there was nothing I could do.

'I'm sorry.'

She hit me across the eye with a can of tuna.

I think I blacked out.

I tumbled backwards into a freezer with Birds Eye Fish Fingers and pizzas and shit.

I could hear Maria screaming and she was thumping my legs and stomach.

People were watching.

The kids started crying.

I managed to crawl out the far side and stepped into someone's trolley.

They had left a child in the seat part and I toppled it over.

The child skidded across the floor and banged its head on a low shelf with raisins.

And I ran.

I ran down aisles of food and drink, past the cash desks, through the car park, through traffic lights, and down rows of houses past pubs.

I jumped on a bus and told the conductor town please.

The bus was packed with weekend shoppers.

I sat down beside a fat lady and knew I had to get pissed.

I went into The Flowing Tide on Abbey Street.

Pint and a short.

And a pint and a short.

Washing the burn of the whiskey away with beer.

My energy was coming back.

I wanted everything to just be okay.

If I could go back in time.

I've never felt so lonely.

I thought about ringing Phil and Declan, but I knew they were doing overtime, and there was no way I was ringing work.

No way.

Pint and a short.

Morning turned to afternoon.

I left to get a bite.

I was numb.

I crossed over by the Abbey down towards the quays.

An itinerant, a big man with short hair was being held on the ground by two guards.

He was crying.

He shouted at a woman 'Don't leave me here, you'll break my heart.'

She was going around the corner with a kid in a pram.

She stopped and shouted something back at him.

I didn't hear what it was but the man let his head fall on the pavement and his body was heaving with sobs.

He was a big man.

After seeing that I needed to get to the south side.

It's nicer.

I was starving.

I love tuna salad, like in a sandwich or a roll. Subs and Salads, South Anne Street.

Straight out of there into Kehoes nearby.

It was pretty full.

I was the only one on my own.

A man at the bar was telling his friends about Monopoly. Everyone goes round the board fifty times or whatever.

And you've made ten grand and you've made two. But look at the board, he said.

The odd hotel or house, but the board's still the same. Nothing's changed and people have made a fortune. What's been bought or sold?

He said it made you think about ownership.

What does it mean to own something?

Something you take for granted.

What does it mean, yours or mine?

It was making me think, so I split.

People tried to sell me stuff on Grafton Street, down Suffolk Street, across Dame Street and into Temple Bar.

I went down to The Norseman and I got lucky.

Phil and Declan had just arrived.

My eye must've been a bit red, they asked me what happened.

I didn't want to talk about it so when they asked how Maria took the news I wriggled out of it.

We got a round.

I found out that Meaney hadn't said anything.

He came to work with his car fixed, and the office window had been repaired that morning.

There was a new terminal on my desk.

We talked about how much better off I was without the job.

The three of us would go into business together. Have a delivery service, driving all around the country with the windows down. And on the continent we'd sleep in the trucks.

They wouldn't let me buy a drink and I suppose that was decent.

I had about ten quid to my name.

I wondered what Maria would do for money.

She probably had some put away.

She was bound to.

There'd be a dinner on the table.

I stopped worrying.

We had toasted sandwiches and plenty of pints.

The evening began to turn and the pub was filling up.

Declan said his girlfriend was in the Stag's Head and we decided to go up.

As we left the Norseman I had a terrible feeling which I can only describe as homesickness.

I suddenly wanted to play with the kids or have a bath with Maria sitting on the toilet talking to me.

I put it down to being drunk.

Get a few more pints inside me and I'd be happy as a pig in shit.

It was ten. Early days. Go home later. Give things a chance to settle for God's sake.

The Stag's Head was black.

People sat in the street drinking.

Declan's girlfriend was downstairs with her Danish friend.

They were wrecked.

We got some pints and everyone was having a laugh, but I just listened and smoked Phil's cigarettes.

I was looking at the punters.

Young people.

Students.

And then I saw this girl.

She was beautiful.

She had long hair past her shoulders.

Straight shiny brown.

I liked the way she was casual.

White sweater, leggings, pair of boots.

She was smoking and talking to some idiot.

He had glasses and was dressed completely in black.

He was all animated talking about a play he was writing about the IRA.

She was just smoking and looking at him.

I thought to myself, if I could be with that girl she could cure my life.

I'd never have to worry about anything – what could go wrong?

At last orders I got a pint and a short.

The place was spinning.

I felt like I was in a big sleeping bag and I was looking at everything through a magnifying glass.

I wanted the lovely girl to look after me.

But I couldn't see her.

The Danish girl said she had tickets for us all to go and see Björn Again at midnight at the Olympia.

The barmen were kicking us out.

One of them shouted at me.

The others didn't notice.

I went upstairs to look for the girl, but she was gone.

I got sick in the street and waited for everyone.

I knew I couldn't go home in this state.

Two blokes asked me if I wanted hash.

I found I couldn't talk very well.

One of them gave me a dig and they started laughing.

I fell over and felt something wet.

It was where I'd been sick.

I think I lay there for a few minutes.

The next thing I remember is Phil picking me up and Declan saying, 'He needs a drink.'

I couldn't think or see straight.

Dame Street moved around my head.

I staggered along between the lads.

The Danish girl wiped my face.

I found it hard to keep my eyes open.

I got sick again and felt a little better. Phil told me I'd have to walk into the Olympia unsupported or none of us would get in.

I walked very slowly past the bouncers pretending to be listening to something Declan's girlfriend was saying.

For some reason I said 'crane operator' and laughed but I can't remember what the joke was now.

The Danish girl handed over the tickets and we were in.

Our seats were upstairs.

The music hadn't started yet.

I fell into my seat and closed my eyes.

Then a cold drink in a paper cup was in my hand.

It was a concoction Declan claimed had power to wake the dead.

A rum and vodka with ice.

I took a gulp and a jolt shot through me.

I was sitting beside Miss Denmark.

Phil was kissing her.

He was licking her face.

One hand was up her skirt and the other one was on her tit.

A bouncer tapped Phil's shoulder and told him to cut it out.

He had to tell a lot of people.

Declan and Siobhan came back with another drink for me and said I looked a lot better.

Well I was awake.

Most of the people there were between thirty and forty.

Civil-servanty types.

Nurses and guards.

Everybody was pissed.

People fell down the stairs or got sick in their seats.

There were a lot of really camp people too.

They spoke loudly and laughed at people they pointed out to each other.

A voice announced that the show involved a strobe light as a warning to people who who took fits.

A man in a yellow T-shirt shouted 'I'm an epileptic, I'm an epileptic.' And everybody laughed.

I didn't think it was very funny.

Björn Again came out and sounded exactly like ABBA. They looked like them and moved like them. It was uncanny.

It was good for about half an hour but the joke wore off and it got boring.

I wandered off to the bar.

I found I still couldn't walk very well – it was hard to keep my balance.

Everything looked like it was on telly.

There was a group of young people down at the front dancing around and having a really good time.

Would they think I was one of the stupid fuckers falling around in my Argyll sweater? Feeling my fat girlfriend's tits in front of everybody?

Didn't they see that I was different?

I wanted to go down on the stage, grab a microphone and scream at everyone that none of what was happening to me was my fault.

I could've done a lot with myself.

I'm an intelligent bloke.

But of course, I didn't.

I got a rum and vodka at the bar after pushing about for ten minutes with housewives and queers.

In the confusion I managed not to pay.

The bar was jammed.

People paying in to drink.

But they had money to burn.

Fat bastards.

And then I saw the girl from The Stag's Head. A man about thirty-five, thirty-six was talking very earnestly to her.

Every now and then she'd smile and shake her head. The man took a step backwards and held out his arms like he wanted her to search him or something.

I leaned against the wall and had a smoke.

I was watching her.

She was gorgeous.

Her skin was really clear, and when she smiled there were creases beside her eyes making her look a lot older.

I figured her for about nineteen or twenty.

Her eyes were wide-set.

Not like she was a mutant or anything.

Just, I can't describe people.

You could see her eyes.

My heart was thumping.

I gulped my drink and moved closer to hear what they were saying.

And when I heard her speak I knew she was the girl for me.

She was experienced, worldly, she could look after me.

The man was talking about his missus.

She was screwing his neighbour.

So it was nothing personal.

He just wanted to get even.

In his own head.

I winced and the girl saw me and smiled.

She smiled at me.

He went on and on.

They could get a hotel room, have a meal.

I made a face. 'Is this guy for real?'

She smiled at me again.

Because she was smiling the bloke thought he had a chance.

She could have a nice breakfast in bed.

A jacuzzi, and come on, he wasn't that bad looking was he? She smiled at me again, then she walked over and held my hand.

She was holding my hand.

The bloke said something about the place being full of lesbians and went back to the bar.

She looked at me and said thanks.

Then she made to go back to the show, but I held her hand and tried speaking to her.

'What?' she was saying, 'what?'

'Cure my life,' I said.

'I want you to cure my life.'

'I think you're beautiful.'

I burst into tears and everyone was looking at me.

She dragged me out of the bar and down to the girls' toilets.

There were some women in there doing their hair and make-up or whatever.

I told them to fuck off before they could tell me I was in the wrong jacks.

We went into a cubicle and she asked me if I was alright.

I couldn't stop crying.

I felt too sorry for myself and I was enjoying it too much.

Poor me . . .

I grabbed her and she gave me a hug.

And inside my head a little voice said, 'Hello . . . nice tits.'

She was asking me what the matter was but I was beginning to feel more horny than upset.

'I'm okay,' I said.

She said we should really get out of there.

Outside we met some of her friends.

Few guys, few girls.

The blokes looked like Bohemian film producers, the girls looked like a bunch of monkeys hooked on crack.

These people were very intense.

Even when they were trying to be funny.

But while she was talking to them she kept holding my hand.

I wasn't feeling horny then.

Just comfortable.

This was all very exciting.

We dumped the losers.

She wanted to know what the matter was but I just asked if we could go.

She didn't say anything.

She just led me down to where her coat was.

Her pals looked at me when she said she was off.

I gave them a moody scowl.

Couldn't they see there was a silent bond, a communication beyond words going on here?

Cunts.

We left the Olympia.

On the way out she squeezed my hand and smiled at me.

She was curing my life.

She hailed a taxi and I bundled in the back.

. . . Yes . . . she got in beside me.

. . . Okay.

She gave the guy an address.

I asked her where she lived.

She said Clontarf.

She lived with her parents but they were away.

'Is that where I'm going?' I asked her.

'Is that where you want to go?' she said.

I put my arm around her and she snuggled into me.

She was slender.

We sped through town.

People tried to flag our taxi.

I saw fights.

Men and women fighting.

Arguments outside chippers.

Drunks asleep in the street.

Down North Strand.

People walking home.

It was starting to rain.

And I was safe in the taxi with the woman I loved.

Through Fairview.

Along the coast.

The tide was out.

Rubbish all along the shore.

Now it was lashing.

I was nice and warm.

We turned left up by Clontarf Castle.

And stopped outside a huge house.

'That's six pounds seven.' The girl paid.

She helped me out of the car.

The front door was a huge slab of oak.

A dark house, smelled musty.

Smelled like the sea.

We were in the sitting room.

Two plush green suites.

Carpets thick as your finger.

Patio doors led to a wide garden. Everything was quiet.

She asked me if I wanted a drink.

A big rum and vodka, with lots of ice.

She had a beer.

We sat there smoking in the lamplight.

'What am I doing here?' I asked her.

'What do you want to do?' she said.

She took my hand and led me upstairs.

A square open landing.

Her door, a room at the back.

A big bed, a table full of books.

Wooden varnished floor.

Her own bathroom en suite.

I asked if I could take a shower.

She said of course.

I locked the door and took a big shit.

I turned on the shower and undressed.

My feet on the tiles.

I saw myself in the mirror.

I looked like I was dead.

Like I'd been beaten to death.

I scrubbed myself from top to bottom.

I was pissed out of my head.

I felt okay.

I dried myself with a nice towel.

My clothes were manky.

I put on her robe and went into the bedroom.

She was in bed.

I was trembling all over.

'You getting in?' she asked me.

I shut the bathroom door and took off the robe.

She pulled back the quilt and I climbed in.

The bed was warm.

She lay on top of me and started kissing my neck.

It was too late now.

My willy went boing.

She laughed and grabbed it.

'What's your name?' I asked her.

'Myfanwy', she said, 'It's Welsh.'

End of Part One.

Part Two

The first thing I remember about waking up is that horrible feeling like you're falling off a cliff.

Everything came flooding back like a kick in the bollocks.

I was lying in a room that shouted money, in bed with a rich girl called Myfanwy.

I checked her bedside clock.

Quarter to ten.

Twelve hours ago I was thinking about going home.

What had happened? The sun was blazing through the window.

Myfanwy was asleep with her back to me.

I could barely remember what she looked like.

I thought about what a slut she was taking a complete stranger to her bed.

The more I thought about it the more disgusted I was.

I'm a married man.

Even if she had no respect for me, at least she should have thought about my wife.

I dozed, and when I looked at the clock again it was eleven.

My head was exploding.

I needed some painkillers or a drink, or both.

My clothes were on the bathroom floor.

I put on her robe and took my stuff downstairs to the washing machine.

I threw everything in except my shoes.

I'm not even going to try describing what kind of shape I was in.

Every movement was an effort.

I found some paracetamol and opened a beer.

Our glasses were where we had left them in the sitting room.

I sat there in someone else's house drinking their beer.

There were photographs on the walls.

Weddings, graduations, black and whites.

I felt like an intruder.

I looked at their videos and their CDs.

I tried playing their piano.

I lay under their coffee table.

They never could have guessed that all the stuff they took for granted would ever receive this much attention.

I was still drunk.

Maria would think I stayed in Phil and Declan's.

I could go home and make it up to her.

I didn't quite know how, but I would.

I was going to sacrifice all my free time and show her I was sorry.

But what was I sorry for? I couldn't go back to my job.

I just couldn't.

She was the one who hit me in Crazy Prices.

I don't think I deserved that.

I didn't know what to do.

I went upstairs.

Myfanwy was still asleep.

I wanted to get out.

I wished I hadn't put my clothes in the machine.

I could've split.

There was a pair of pink tracksuit bottoms on the back of a chair.

I put them on and got a pair of tiny socks out of a drawer.

I found a T-shirt and got my shoes.

The sun was baking down.

I left the door on the latch, and strolled up the road.

I went around by the cricket club and down Belgrove Road as far as Vernon Avenue.

Then I turned right.

Down to the seafront.

Clontarf is beautiful.

Old houses and trees, the breeze comes over the sea, and there's a ghost on every corner.

People were coming and going to mass.

I went down the coast and into the Dollymount house.

It was huge. A boozerama.

I got a pint and a short and sat at a window looking at the bay curving round to Howth.

You could see everything clearly.

It was peaceful.

I wished I was on top of Howth Head, looking at Dublin.

I wished it was a couple of years ago and I was making plans instead of just drifting with whatever went on.

I had another pint and it made a huge difference.

I felt much better.

I had about four quid to my name.

I knew I wanted to get pissed before holy hour so I mooched back along the coast to Myfanwy's road.

I heard a radio in the kitchen when I pushed the big front door open.

'Is that you?' she shouted.

'Yeah.' I said, because I'm witty like that.

She bounded to the kitchen door and looked out at me.

She started laughing and told me my clothes would be ready soon.

She asked me if I was hungry.

I said a sandwich would be fine.

We sat in the kitchen for a while.

She gave me a can of beer and asked me where I'd gone.

When I told her she said I drink too much. She wanted to know who was playing the piano at the crack of dawn.

I said it wasn't me, and she said no, it was nice.

She started asking me about myself.

She didn't even know my name.

I said it was Michael.

She wanted to know where I lived and worked.

I couldn't answer her.

I knew she had her suspicions, but I'm a coward and I asked her questions instead.

She'd been a student at Trinity.

She had a degree in Italian and something else.

She was going to do a business diploma.

I asked her if she had a hangover.

She said she hadn't been drinking.

For some reason I found that perverse.

I told her I wanted to go into town.

She gave my clothes a shot in the dryer.

I had another beer and ate my sandwich.

I didn't feel like talking much.

She sat on my lap and started kissing me but I didn't feel much like that either.

She said I'd changed my tune since last night, and did I not think she was beautiful any more?

Of course, talking about last night she might as well have been talking about the Boer War as far as I held myself responsible.

I told her I was tired and maybe later.

But her parents were coming home later she said.

I know this seems shitty, but if I was going to get pissed I had to stay on her good side and time was ticking away.

I spent half an hour banging her on the sitting-room floor.

Then she ironed my pants and I was going mad because it was half one.

We'd never make it in time.

She laughed and said we'd take her car.

She had a fucking car.

She turned on the alarm and took her Mini out of the garage.

Zoom.

She was a pretty good driver.

We were sitting in Davy Byrne's (her choice) at ten to two.

We both had pints.

Then I had a pint and a short.

Then I had another pint and Myfanwy had a glass. She paid. She knew.

We were finally kicked out at half two.

That felt much better.

And only another hour and a half till the next one.

Myfanwy asked if I was okay.

'Oh yeah, fine.'

She asked what I wanted to do now.

I didn't mind.

We walked around for a while.

Around Merrion Square and St Stephen's Green.

She asked me questions.

At the start when I wouldn't answer she thought it was sort of fun, but I could see it was beginning to annoy her now.

She was bored with the mystery man.

I felt rotten about it.

We sat down in a place on South Anne Street for something to eat.

I told her everything that had happened over the last two days.

She was excited.

She liked me.

I impressed her.

She didn't mind that I was married or anything.

I told her about my daughters.

But then I had to stop.

It was none of her fucking business.

She wanted to know if there was anything she could do.

I said, 'No . . . just keep paying.'

She laughed and put her arms around me. After she had held on to me for a minute she looked at me but although she was smiling she was a bit tearful for some reason.

I suppose it was a bit sad.

It was still very warm so we took our coffee outside.

We sat at a table like garden furniture and she said she thought I should ring my wife.

But I was too embarrassed and guilty.

She wanted to know if she could see me again. I didn't know.

Anyway she said, we had the rest of the day.

There was a party in Rathmines that night and would I go.

Of course, I said I would.

Anything to avoid thinking about going home just yet.

Then a group of Myfanwy's friends came along.

Everybody wanted to hug Myfanwy.

I think they reckoned I was just someone sitting at her table.

They seemed a bit surprised when she introduced me.

There was Rupert, a huge bloke who looked like an officer in the SS.

Feargal, a squatty little guy with glasses that had a cord going round the back of his neck.

Sorcha, who looked like a model.

Jane, who had a complexion like dark cream.

And Sinead who spoke Irish as much as she could.

They all got coffee.

My buzz was wearing off but Myfanwy seemed to want to stay there.

Rupert was at acting school.

His class were doing a modern version of *King Oedipus* and everybody had to go.

He had learned so much about himself since the start of rehearsals.

There's nothing in modern drama that isn't in Greek tragedy and comedy.

I asked him what the theatre had to do with real life.

I thought he'd have an answer seeing as he was at a school and everything.

But he went on for about ten minutes and it was very boring.

I can't remember what he said.

Then he started to explain why comedy is funny breaking it down into some Russian cunt's three 'levels' of humour.

No one laughed.

He kept touching Myfanwy's hand.

I wanted for me and her to go and get sloshed.

Sorcha was a model.

She had done an ad for shampoo where no one saw her face, just the back of her head.

Then a fight broke out when Feargal said he thought Christy Turlington looked like a baboon.

They talked about Rwanda.

Friends of theirs abroad.

A girl they knew was pregnant.

A lecturer at Trinity who wore pink cords.

They spoke about how the country would never forgive Dick Spring for going into government with Albert.

And I wanted a pint.

I knew I was as intelligent as these fuckers.

But I just didn't seem to have any opinions.

I was embarrassed sitting there.

I eventually got the nerve to ask Myfanwy to come for a drink.

To my dismay, everyone thought this was a great idea.

We went to the International Bar.

Going down Grafton Street and Wicklow Street Myfanwy held my hand.

I was shitting someone I knew would see me.

I wasn't enjoying myself.

I sat back in the pub and let Myfanwy do the buying.

She did the necessary.

She was curing my life.

Her friends drank a pint an hour.

Myfanwy and I drank steadily.

Pace is the secret.

I was feeling a little better.

I was talking to Jane, the girl with the complexion like dark cream.

I told her a joke about niggers and she lost the head.

I didn't talk to her again.

And then Feargal and her left to collect Feargal's kid from his ex-girlfriend.

I asked Sorcha if being a model meant people treated her like a bimbo, or a good-looking object.

She said no and I didn't pursue it.

I was bored.

Myfanwy got me a rum and vodka.

Rupert told us about a film script he was writing with a friend of his from college.

It was about a girl who wants to be an artist but lacks the confidence.

He wanted to set it in Paris and have it done in French.

It would be more beautiful.

I asked if he spoke French.

He said not really but it was going to be subtitled.

I didn't understand, but he'd had three pints so I let it go.

He told us he found women more interesting than men.

He wanted to be a woman.

He wasn't gay or anything.

He just thought women have better insights and if they ran things the world wouldn't be as fucked up.

I told him I thought he was a prick.

But Myfanwy laughed and the others thought it was a joke.

It turned out to be Rupert's party we were going to.

They left for his house to get things ready.

It was dusk and the pub was nearly empty.

Myfanwy put her head on my shoulder and told me she didn't know what to say.

I told her that was alright, because I wasn't interested anyway.

She laughed and held me.

Then we got up and went out to her Mini.

We stopped on George Street and Myfanwy gave me a fiver to get fags.

I bought two packs.

Camel Lights and Gauloises.

I was being a classy guy I explained to Myfanwy.

'Mmm . . . ' she said, 'Mind if we take a detour?'

We drove to Ranelagh and stopped outside a house Myfanwy said was her brother's.

She was going to dress me properly.

Her brother was in Pakistan writing a history textbook.

We went up to his bedroom.

She opened the huge wardrobe and started throwing things onto the bed.

Hundreds of pounds' worth of shirts.

A jacket that cost five hundred pounds.

A tie that cost seventy pounds.

And that's what I'm wearing now.

I don't think it does much for me but it felt classy at the time.

While I was standing there half-undressed Myfanwy started feeling me up.

I knew what I had to do and I did it.

We were back in the car at ten.

I took a bottle of vodka from her brother's drink cabinet.

We could hear the music coming from Rupert's house from down the road where we were parked.

He had the house to himself and there were people in every window.

We walked in past people drinking in the garden.

A couple were snogging in the hall.

We went into the kitchen.

Myfanwy was talking to some friends of hers in the doorway.

I sat at the kitchen table and poured some vodka into a mug.

A bunch of lads from the country asked for a sup.

I passed them the bottle and they slugged out of it.

Some blokes over at the back door kept going out for a joint.

I don't think they were afraid of being caught, they just didn't want to share it.

Another bloke was standing at the cooker making himself some soup.

A girl stood behind him with her hands in his front pockets.

Two girls and a bloke stood in front of me at the table talking about films I'd never heard of.

I went to have a look around.

The music was all techno.

There were people in the living room going mad to it.

MTV was on with the sound down.

Myfanwy was dancing.

She looked fabulous.

She had a sleeveless check shirt and a pair of shorts.

Rupert was dancing like he'd just been let out of a mental home.

A young couple sat on the floor in a corner.

They were having a shit time.

The girl made half-arsed attempts to get her boyfriend up to dance but you could see neither of them really wanted to.

I sat down with them and we shared the bottle.

The girl took a smoke.

I wanted to know what was wrong with them.

I wanted them to relax and cheer up. It sort of became important to me.

They kept saying they were alright but I knew they were fucked.

What was it about them?

I don't know.

'I hope it'll be okay,' I said.

'That's all I'm going to say to you.'

I went to pour them more drink but the bottle was gone.

We looked around.

Someone had taken it.

Then the girl saw it.

The muckers from the country had it.

They were sitting on the couch talking to a very beautiful girl.

If they had asked I would've given them some.

The girl said she was going to ask them to give it back.

'No,' I said, 'Don't ask.'

I stood up and bent over the couple. I shook the guy's hand and kissed the girl on her forehead.

I was a bit upset.

I went over to the couch.

The muckers looked at me.

One of them had the bottle between his legs trying to hide it.

I grabbed it away from him and swung it at his face.

The bottom of it hit his nose right on the bridge.

That really fucked up his face.

The bottle hadn't smashed so I heaved it against the side of another bloke's head.

It broke with a pop and glass went everywhere.

Someone screamed.

I went to find Myfanwy.

We were going.

She wasn't in the kitchen or out the back.

She wasn't on the stairs or in the toilet.

There was no one in the first bedroom. A pair of eejits were playing guitars in the next one.

The lights were off in the third.

Bad news.

I found the switch.

Myfanwy was on the bed.

Her shirt was open and her shorts were around her feet.

Rupert's head was between her legs.

He was kneeling on the floor pulling himself off.

The first thought that went through my head was 'He's licking my spunk.'

Myfanwy saw me and started kicking him away.

But he kept a hold of her.

I started laughing.

He lifted his head up and said 'Squeeze your tits, I'm coming.'

He saw me and came.

Myfanwy rolled over and put her head in her hands.

Rupert pulled the quilt off the bed and covered himself.

'Goodbye.' I said.

The lights were all on downstairs and the music had stopped.

People brought towels in and out of the living room.

I saw Myfanwy's jacket on a chair beside the hall phone.

I took her wallet and left.

The night was warm.

Myfanwy had twenty quid.

I hailed a taxi and said, 'Raheny please.'

'You were walking the wrong way mate,' he said.

We drove through town, through Fairview, up the Howth road, across Sibyl Hill and into Raheny village.

'This is fine,' I said.

I was hungry so I went over to the chipper.

It was about twelve o'clock and the chipper was packed.

There were two men in front of me who were about forty.

They were wrecked.

One of them had a little girl with him who was about two.

She was sleepy and crying.

He was asking her if she wanted chips.

Then he told his friend he was dead.

His missus would kill him.

I didn't feel hungry after that.

I made my way back to the estate.

One or two people were walking back from the pub.

All the houses the same.

Each one with a mortgage.

Each one with a love story.

I opened the front door quietly and crept upstairs.

Everything was like a tomb.

I went into my daughters.

I sat on the floor and listened to them breathing.

Their fair hair and white-cotton pyjamas.

Their little hands.

I couldn't bear it.

THE GOOD THIEF

For Kevin Hely

The Good Thief was first performed under the title *The Light of Jesus* by Fly by Night Theatre Company at the City Arts Centre, Dublin, on 18 April 1994.

Performer   Kevin Hely
Director   Conor McPherson
Slide photography   Paul Kinsella

It was subsequently performed as a Loopline production, as part of the Dublin Theatre Festival on 4 October 1994.

Performer   Garrett Keogh
Director   Conor McPherson
Designer   Anne Layde
Slide photography   Robbie Ryan

Let's begin with an incident.

I was sitting in Joe Murray's bar one night, as I usually did.

I was talking to this couple I liked and having a few beers.

I was working for Joe Murray at this time as a paid thug.

I scared people for him.

Set fire to places.

Shot people. As warnings.

My girlfriend Greta had just left me but I still saw her most days because she had left me for Joe Murray.

Power attracts women.

Also, I had been beating her up and I knew it was wrong but I'm not the issue here, so let's leave it.

Let's not. She annoyed me.

She gave herself to any man who wanted it. I knew this for a fact and I was sick of sticking it where someone else had had it a few hours ago.

Anyway, I was having a few glasses of beer with this couple I really liked and relaxing.

That day I'd had to chase a man up and down his premises in Capel Street.

He knew all these stairwells and stuff you wouldn't think were there.

I was exhausted.

He was a shoe repairman.

I hate people with skills who can do stuff.

It's a small quibble but I refuse to constrain my personality.

I believe that that can lead to problems.

I must've broken every bone in his hands.

Then I shaved his head and kicked his nuts so many times he passed out.

This couple I was talking to were young and funny.

They came in and out sometimes.

They were friendly with each other too.

I was a little bit jealous of them but I was happy for them at the same time.

I was just having a few glasses of beer and we were chatting about politics and movies and the weather and stuff.

I saw Greta over the other side of the bar talking to Harry Delaney, a man who'd been living in England for a number of years and wore a necklace.

I felt like tossing my drink over at them but I was in too good a mood.

The couple I was talking to bought me a drink and I bought them one and we were talking about clothes and style.

Greta walked past me and didn't look.

She had her coat on and she was smoking.

I saw Harry Delaney shoot back his drink and go the long way round.

I knew what they were doing.

I was going mad but fuck them, I thought.

It was a cold night.

They'd have to do it in the car park.

They'd freeze their bare arses off.

And Greta would have to be back at closing time to suck Joe Murray's dick. Or whatever it was she did after hours.

I'm probably not being very fair.

But life's not fair.

So she was gone out with Harry Delaney and she was gone a few minutes.

I was shooting the breeze with this young couple I really liked and Joe Murray comes downstairs and starts looking around.

The look on his face made my day.

When he saw that Greta wasn't there he looked miserable and annoyed at the same time.

You see, I knew he loved Greta.

He was the type of man who would've put her in a china cabinet and polish her if he could.

But I knew what he liked.

He liked putting it up girls' arses and I'd seen him do it.

He was a right degenerate.

This was one of the things annoyed me about him and Greta. She probably enjoyed it. I always preferred it straight.

I'm not a messer.

He was looking around and people were talking to him. Asking him for favours or spoofing him he'd lost weight.

Eventually I heard him ask somebody where Greta was, but no one had seen her go out.

He came around to us and I introduced everyone. The young couple were leaving.

I said I'd see them again and it was nice talking to them.

Murray bought me a drink and began talking a bit of business.

But I knew he was going to talk to me about Greta.

He had never squared it with me, the way she'd moved out of our place and into his.

I knew that if he mentioned it, it would annoy me too much.

He asked me had I seen her.

I said I had but I didn't know where she was.

Then it was sort of funny.

He said, 'Does she do this much? I mean go off without saying anything?'

I thought it was gas. Him asking me this.

It was very bad manners but I answered him anyway and said I didn't know.

I could see he knew he shouldn't have asked me for advice after taking her away from me. But sometimes he was as thick as shit. He really was.

Yeah.

Well. That's the incident I wanted to begin with. It's sort of funny, isn't it? Kind of sick as well.

There's just something not quite right about it. Hard to put your finger on though.

Anyway, something about it changed the way I felt about Joe Murray and the way I felt probably contributed to the mayhem that happened over the next few days.

And that's what I really want to talk about.

So that night I had a couple of beers after closing with Joe Murray and Vinnie Rourke, an old-time vicious bastard who'd done fifteen years for armed robbery.

I didn't speak to him much and I'd heard he had 'mellowed with age'.

But I knew he was a psycho and that he did odd jobs for Murray when he wanted a real pro and not a messy bastard like me.

Greta came back and Murray was asking her where she'd been and where Harry Delaney was. But she didn't answer him. She just poured herself a big tequila and lit a cigarette.

Vinnie Rourke and a little fucker who followed him everywhere, Seamus Parker, were looking at her like they wanted to give her one each. Or at the same time.

Joe Murray always seemed weak when Greta was around.

I was imagining Murray doing it to her and her loving it. It disgusted me but I couldn't get it out of my head.

I had to bang a couple of shorts away.

I was messing with the jukebox, putting The Beatles on.

Murray came over and gave me a piece of paper with an address on it. It was a man called Mitchell who owned a number of warehouses which he leased to food importers mostly. But we also knew that from time to time he'd hold on to dodgy gear from some of the bigger robberies in the city. Antiques and that.

Murray had been threatening to set fire to Mitchell's warehouses for years.

This brought in about a grand and a half a month, but with the recession Mitchell was asking for some leeway.

Murray had refused and Mitchell was giving it all this guff about some second cousin in the IRA getting on to it.

My job was to go round to his house and scare him.

I told Murray okay and he gave me a hundred as a sub.

Back at the bar, Vinnie Rourke was staring at me. I knew that he didn't like Murray giving me work for some reason.

But I did my best to ignore him and put plenty of effort into drinking Greta out of my head.

It got hazy after that and I just remember driving home wishing I was more drunk.

When I woke up it was about nine and I had a blinder of a hangover.

I considered not doing the job for Murray but he had given me a sub and that meant it was important to him.

I did a trick from my days as a second lieutenant which always fooled my body into action.

First I took some aspirin and then some Vivioptal tablets which are a tonic, giving you energy after you've been sick, then a Valium, and then I put the kettle on.

I ran a cold bath while I shaved, then I stripped and hitting the water was like being born. Everything went mad. I put my head under the water and blew bubbles.

Then I stood up and let my body get warm before sliding under for another shock.

I was shivering while I dried myself.

I made a huge hot whiskey with lemon and cloves and it blew the roof off my head.

Made me drunk very quickly.

I had another one and then I checked my guns.

The shotgun I had was beautifully handmade by a man in Mullingar, but of course I'd ruined it by sawing the barrel in half.

It was lethal and it often frightened me to carry it. I was always worried it would go off.

I also had a very old, very beautiful Webley Revolver which was more just in case. I was told that this one I had was used to give the coup de grâce to deserters in France. I never knew if that was true.

It was accurate up to about sixty yards and it was so pristine I doubted it had ever seen action.

It was starting to rain as I got into the car. I wanted to get this over with quickly before my hangover caught up with me.

There was only old tat on the radio but I kept it on for company.

When I was nearly there I took my bag of gear out.

I had a balaclava for extra frighteners and an industrial anorak because only mentlers wear them as everyday jackets.

The address I wanted was in a new estate where everything looked a bit pokey.

Looking back, I don't know why I put a cartridge in the shotgun.

My revolver was always loaded and I had it in the back of my jeans.

But I never trusted the shotgun.

I had very few cartridges anyway.

Maybe I wanted to make some noise if this Mitchell guy knew how to take care of himself.

I'll never know, but it was one of the luckiest things I ever did.

I pulled on the balaclava and put the shotgun inside my jacket.

I thought I saw a curtain move upstairs but I wasn't sure.

I was ringing for about a minute when the door opened.

And there was a bloke in a balaclava.

He hit me in the face with a heavy cosh and grabbed my arm as I went for the shotgun.

He pulled me into the hall and kicked me on the back of the head.

I lay trying to get a grip on the radiator.

He slammed the door.

I heard a gun bolt and somebody said, 'Don't move.'

I froze.

My balaclava was pulled off and I was turned around.

My shotgun was on the hall table.

The man who'd grabbed me was standing in front of me and there was another one in overalls on the stairs holding an automatic rifle.

I knew this was out of my league and I was terrified.

I could see into the kitchen. Mitchell, who I was supposed to be scaring, was there with his wife and a little girl of about three or four.

Well, they were scared anyway.

The man on the stairs asked if Joe Murray had sent me and I immediately said yes, but that I was only there to threaten everybody.

The two men laughed at this and I laughed too.

I was hoping to make friends with them so they'd let me go. I know how stupid that sounds but these were professionals and they didn't give a shit.

The stairs man said they weren't going to kill me.

'Thanks,' I said, and meant it.

He was all business and told me I was going to be shot in the legs, but they were afraid of ricochets so would I go out the back and lie on the grass?

I couldn't believe it.

Mitchell said something in the kitchen about not wanting them to do it there.

He was fat and baldy. The woman looked petrified.

The stairs man got annoyed and said, 'What do you want us to fucking do? We can't drive around like this.'

'What do I tell the guards?' said Mitchell.

The stairs man told him I couldn't go to the guards. They'd dump me miles away.

They argued about the noise gunshots would make.

The one in front of me suggested they use a sledgehammer on my legs.

They seemed to agree.

Mitchell was told to clear out for a few hours and take his missus with him.

And I was making up something you couldn't call a plan.

I didn't want to be a cripple for the rest of my life. I knew I'd have to pull the pistol from my pants and start shooting.

This was all pure panic.

The stairs man told Mitchell to go out the back way. But Mitchell said his keys were in the living room.

As he walked down the hall to the door beside me I grabbed the Webley and fired it straight ahead. I didn't bother taking aim. The shot hit the man in front of me in the hip and he collapsed on top of me, knocking the pistol on to the floor.

Then the stairs man started shooting.

He hit the living-room door jamb and the wall before getting Mitchell in the back. And then there was a clicking sound.

His rifle had jammed.

An empty cartridge was stuck in the breach and he was trying to release it by working the bolt back and forth.

I was on my knees and I pulled the shotgun from the hall table.

I saw the empty cartridge fly out of his gun and he accidentally fired a shot into the banister.

I pointed the shotgun up the stairs, and without being sure I had cocked or even fired, it discharged a deafening shot.

The man jerked backwards up the stairs and landed sitting at the bathroom door.

I knew he was dead.

I hit the man in the hall over the head with the gun till he lay still, then I rolled him over and took my pistol.

Mitchell was still alive. He was shaking and losing a lot of blood.

His wife was trying to unlock the back door and keep her child in front of her.

I dragged her back and the child hung on.

I got them on to the floor and told them to shut up.

I slapped the woman on the neck. I meant to hit her face but I was shaking.

She quietened down and I told her I wasn't going to hurt them.

Then my legs went from under me.

My knees just buckled and I was on the floor beside them.

There was a phone on the worktop and I was trying to remember Joe Murray's number. When I got through, he wasn't in the bar. It took ages for them to get him.

He couldn't believe what had happened.

He told me to keep the woman and the kid there and not to do anything.

He was sending someone over.

The woman wasn't moving. She just held her kid, who seemed to be asleep.

I went through to the hall.

Mitchell was still breathing but it was a funny sound.

His face was pressed against the hinge of the half-opened door.

I thought there was blood coming out of his mouth.

Upstairs the dead man was still holding his rifle. He was sitting in a shower of pellet wounds.

Most of them were in his chest and shoulder but a few were in his neck and one or two in his face.

I took the magazine from his gun.

It was only a matter of time before the noise brought the guards to the house.

I decided to keep my options open.

The first sign of trouble I was getting out as fast as I could.

I took Mitchell's keys from the living room and went into the kitchen.

I asked Mrs Mitchell if she was alright.

She just nodded and didn't look at me.

The kid looked drugged.

The kitchen had every modern appliance and for some reason that made me sad.

I was impatient. I wanted to get out.

I was watching Mitchell. He was breathing in shallow gasps.

The other man in the hall began to move a little bit. I told him to stay where he was. 'What are you going to do?' he asked me. I told him some friends of mine were coming and he could explain his side of it to the guards while I was miles away having a pint.

Then he said it. 'They're going to kill you.'

Now whether he meant his buddies or mine, I didn't know. But I began to worry.

How the fuck did these guys know I'd be coming that morning? Vinnie Rourke didn't like me and Joe Murray would more than likely send him.

And I'd made a pig's mickey of this.

Mrs Mitchell could identify me and sooner or later they'd trace me back to Murray. Mrs Mitchell was in trouble and I was in trouble. One of us would have to go.

I was watching the street. Across the road a woman was standing in her porch.

She'd heard something, but she didn't seem to know what to do. She went back inside and a car pulled up. The driver kept it running. Vinnie Rourke and two others got out. One of them looked into my car and nodded at Rourke. He adjusted something in his jacket and walked towards the house.

I just knew.

I ran into the kitchen and shouted at Mrs Mitchell to tell me where their car was.

It was in a garage out the back.

I heard the doorbell.

I ran down the garden and smashed the garage door open.

Mitchell's car was huge, a Rover, and the lane at the back of the house was narrow.

I heard shouting from the house and I thought about just legging it through the gardens. I stood in the garage and I couldn't decide what to do.

Then someone came out the back and called my name. It was Chris Breen, an old buddy of Vinnie Rourke's. He saw me.

He was holding a small pistol.

'Where are you going?' he said, 'Come back.'

I didn't move.

'We've got to get out of here,' he said.

I stepped into the garden.

'What'll we do with the woman and the kid?' I asked him.

'Just come back in,' he said.

I kept my hand on the butt of my revolver and pointed it at him through my jacket.

And we went back into the house.

Rourke's other mate, who I didn't know, had gagged Mrs Mitchell and he was tying her hands behind her back.

The little girl was trying to cling to her mother. The man looked up from what he was doing and nodded at me.

Rourke was in the hall, strangling the man I'd wounded.

When he finished he stood up and looked at me. 'This is a fucking mess,' he said, 'and I like the witnesses.' He nodded at Mrs Mitchell. Chris Breen was pointing his gun at me.

'What are you doing?' I said.

He smiled and shrugged at me.

I shot him through my pocket and ran backwards, slamming the kitchen door on Rourke.

The one I didn't know put his hands up.

Chris Breen was sitting on the floor.

I'd got him in the mouth. He was looking around like this was the first stuff he'd ever seen. I heard the front door as Rourke ran out to the car.

'Lean over the sink,' I told Rourke's friend, 'Put your head in the sink. If you move, I'll kill you,' I told him.

I picked Mrs Mitchell up and pushed her out the back. The kid clung to her leg.

I got them down to the garage and into the back of the car. Mrs Mitchell lay across the back seat and the kid tumbled on to the floor.

The car was an automatic.

I had to keep my head to manoeuvre it into the lane.

I nudged it little by little and the lane opened up on to a road that ran around a green and then out to what looked like a main road.

I began to feel relieved, even jokey.

I asked Mrs Mitchell if she wanted the radio on, and it seemed so ridiculous I started laughing. I was laughing and driving and I didn't know where I was going.

All I could think about was getting back to Greta and taking her away from Joe Murray. We could start again.

Then I heard sirens and knew we had to get out of the city.

We drove along Sundrive Road and Dolphin Road. Long roads with houses, garages, shops, undertakers, estate agents.

Eventually we hit the N4.

The sun was glinting in the rearview mirror. The eleven o'clock news had nothing yet. By lunchtime it'd be all over the place.

I pulled into a lay-by and shut the engine off. I leaned back and rubbed my face.

My hangover was coming back. I had hot flushes and shivers.

I got out and listened to the rain soaking into the ground, the odd car going past.

I bent over and got sick. The smell of whiskey and sugar made me retch again.

I knew I had to talk to Mrs Mitchell, get her on my side. Buy us some time.

When I got myself together, I went back to the car. Mrs Mitchell's head was against the door and the kid had climbed up on the seat beside her. She had a little blue dress on and one of her shoes was off.

Her hair was the same colour as her mother's but her face was chubbier.

Mrs Mitchell was very thin.

Her hands looked sore from the clothes line that tied them.

Her tracksuit bottoms were half off and I could have seen anything I wanted, but it just made me feel sick.

The kid was looking at me and Mrs Mitchell was gasping for air.

There was snot all over her face and the rag around her mouth was soaking.

'Now Mrs Mitchell,' I said, 'I'm going to talk to you and when you hear what I have to say, I'm going to untie you, do you understand me?' She nodded.

'When I untie you there's nowhere to run and I don't think you will if you listen to what I'm going to tell you. Can I trust you about these things?' She nodded again.

I sat in the driver's seat and began.

'Now listen, very soon the guards will be looking everywhere for us. There'll be roadblocks. I can't give you up because you can identify me. The men who came to your house were going to kill me and they were going to kill you.

They'll have gotten out of there without leaving a whole lot of clues. They're old-time convicted rogues and they know what they're doing.

I'm in no position to go to the police and neither are you.

You knew what was going to happen to me and you didn't do anything.'

She shook her head and made a noise.

I told her I'd take her gag off in a minute and she could say what she liked then. I told her I'd only come to scare her husband and that everything else was his fault, except for the bunch of cunts I worked for.

'Now I have no intention of hurting you,' I told her. 'It was the men your husband hired who shot him. It was an accident.'

I made it clear I didn't want any of this but if we kept our heads and worked together we might live to tell the tale.

Joe Murray was sure to send Vinnie Rourke after us in case I blabbed to the guards as some sort of bargain.

He'd want Mrs Mitchell too because she might link me to Murray.

Whoever the men who tried to break my legs were, if they were terrorists, their pals would be coming after us and of course, every guard in every shitty little fuckhole would have his eyes peeled.

She simply had to cooperate.

I asked her if she understood.

When she nodded, I leaned forward and took off the gag.

Then I pushed her up and undid her hands.

She sat up and held her kid.

'Thank you,' she said.

I didn't feel like talking any more.

'We've got to change this car,' I said, 'Next town, we're changing this car.'

Then she said she didn't know what was going to happen at the house.

Mitchell's friends had come a few minutes before me. She didn't know who they were or what was going on.

I didn't say anything.

I just drove.

The news had been about a shooting and a possible kidnapping.

It was good being patchy. Right now the guards would be trying to figure out where Mrs Mitchell might be without all the big search stuff.

She could be at the shops for all they knew.

Vinnie Rourke and the others must've gotten away. There were plenty of doctors Joe Murray knew who'd look after Chris Breen.

I reckoned Mr Mitchell was dead.

I didn't say anything about it.

Mrs Mitchell had her daughter on her lap. Things were peaceful.

I was beginning to see how lucky I'd been. Lucky or stupid.

I wondered which was worse, broken legs or being chased for killing someone.

Well I hadn't been caught, so maybe this was better.

I wanted to know what Greta would think.

This had to put me back at the centre of her thoughts. I wanted to know if she was worried about me. Did she think I was a fucking idiot?

Then I thought about Joe Murray putting it up her arse.

I called her a fucking bitch and apologised to Mrs Mitchell. I hadn't meant her. I hadn't meant her at all.

We drove into Kinnegad and I parked behind Jack's Bar, cum-restaurant-B&B.

I asked Mrs Mitchell if she wanted to get cleaned up.

She said okay. Then she asked me how I was for money.

I had about forty quid which wasn't going to get us very far.

She told me to take a map out of the glove compartment. There was a banklink card in the map. The name on it was Patrick Mitchell. 'Do you know the number?' I stupidly asked her.

She just took it.

We left the car there.

This was her chance. If she wanted one.

All she had to do was grab someone or make a run for it. I didn't know if she had enough reasons to trust me. Or if she was afraid of me.

But we found a vending machine and she withdrew two hundred quid.

For someone who'd just seen her husband shot she was remarkably calm.

'Maybe it's shock,' I thought.

She picked the girl up in her lean arms and we went into Harry's, another bar down the street.

I told them to go and get cleaned up and not be too long about it.

It was twenty to one and some lunch people were sitting about. The more the better as far as I was concerned. I sank a pint and got another one. I knew I had to slow down. I didn't need the attention. I sat at the window and pretended to read a paper someone had left there.

A Bus Éireann bus had stopped across the street. The driver was helping a woman get her luggage from the side.

I ordered sandwiches and tea and soup.

Then I thought about the girl and got chips and ice cream. I drank a small one and it calmed me down. Took the edge off.

Mrs Mitchell seemed hungry which I also thought was really odd.

The kid ate the ice cream then the chips.

Mrs Mitchell was dipping her sandwiches in her soup. I got her a brandy and she drank it.

She called the kid Monkey. 'Taste this, Monkey, wipe your hands.' The kid was very quiet and well-behaved. Mrs Mitchell asked where we should go.

I had a friend who lived in Sligo, Jeff.

He owned an estate agents.

I thought he could give us somewhere to put our heads down for a few days, watch the news. See which way the guards jumped. How much they knew about her husband or if they linked the whole thing to Murray.

She didn't say whether she thought it was a good idea or not. Which was good enough for me. I told them to wait.

And I went out to look for an old-style Fiesta. These were cars I could start with very little hassle.

There was one outside the Post Office but there were too many people. I went the other way to where the road turns left at the end of the town.

There was a car park in front of some offices and a big factory.

I saw a woman get out of a 1981 Fiesta.

This was no bother.

I took out my keys and pretended to be wiping the windscreen of a Suzuki van.

When she was gone I went over and wrapped a stone in my jacket. I smashed the rear fly window on the driver's side.

When I reached in the fucking thing was open already. That's the country.

I kicked the cover off the steering column and pulled the wires out of the ignition lock. I got it going in a couple of seconds and drove around in front of Harry's.

Mrs Mitchell didn't make a fuss. She just came out and got in.

I was surprised. She got in the front.

I told them to be careful of the glass and then we U-turned and headed west again.

Mrs Mitchell wanted to know what we'd do if we came across a roadblock.

We decided to pretend we were married.

'What's your name?' I asked the girl.

She didn't answer me.

'Niamh,' said Mrs Mitchell.

'Hello Niamh,' I said.

'Hello,' said Niamh.

We caught the headlines at half one.

Three bodies had been found in the house but hadn't been identified.

Mrs Mitchell just looked out the window.

The traffic was heavy coming through Mullingar.

The rain came down in sheets.

I was relaxing. There wouldn't be roadblocks this far out.

I felt safe when we went through Longford without any hassle.

I was thinking about my friend, Jeff who'd moved to Boyle a few years before any of this.

He sold houses and land in Sligo, Leitrim, Roscommon. We'd only seen each other once or twice since he'd moved.

I'd stayed with him in a house no one was buying, on the Shannon.

Greta had come and we drank and went out in a boat, all that sort of stuff.

Jeff had a wife and four kids, but he was very laid-back. I trusted him and I hoped he could sort us out.

He knew what I did for a living and one time I'd helped him out.

A local councillor called Burke had hinted that Jeff would have to pay what he called an 'an administration fee' of five grand for planning permission for two bungalows Jeff was building for some people in Dublin.

Jeff said this was bollocks and told the councillor to fuck off.

A couple of nights later while Jeff was having a piss in the pub, someone punched him on the back of the head.

He broke a front tooth on the tiling.

He got a few kicks and someone told him to get his responsibility as a citizen together. And all that tat.

This told him that Burke must have been behind it.

He phoned me in Dublin.

He was scared. He wanted Burke off his back but didn't want to know the details.

I drove to Boyle on a Tuesday afternoon.

Burke spent his afternoons in a pub called The Riverside. He drank with men who worked for him. Delivering peat briquettes.

They watched the telly for racing results.

Burke never spoke to anyone unless they spoke to him.

I watched him mill five or six pints and when I saw him get ready to go I slipped out in front of him.

I followed him home. He drove a Mercedes.

He lived across from his farm which was a series of fields along a bend in the river. It was a nice spot.

I sat and waited, enjoying the peace and quiet. I wanted to make sure he was alone. He had no children. His wife left the house around five. She was a nurse.

A few minutes later, Burke came out with wellies and a walking stick.

He went down to the river and looked at the bank. There was some flooding.

I got out and waved at him.

He turned and waved back.

I walked towards him with a friendly smile.

He gripped his stick a little tighter and watched me carefully. He was much bigger than me and I knew I'd have to fuck him up very quickly.

When I was about fifteen feet away from him, I started to say 'I wonder if you could tell me where I might find a place called . . . '

And I kicked the shit out of him.

I kicked him as he tried to run away.

I kicked him on the ground and I hit him with his stick until I was exhausted.

Then I picked him up and punched and dragged him back up to his house.

He collapsed on the driveway but I kicked his arse and got him inside.

'Where's the kitchen?' I asked him.

'I don't have any money here,' he said.

I told him to shut up.

I didn't want to tell him Jeff had sent me in case Burke's friends did something to him.

I wanted to fuck him up generally so that he'd be too scared to do anything to anybody. And I wanted him in the kitchen because that's where people keep their knives.

Mrs Mitchell wanted to use the toilet so we stopped in Carrick on Shannon.

The news had that one of the dead men had been identified as Dublin businessman, Patrick Mitchell.

The Gardai were interviewing witnesses at the scene.

A woman had seen three men come out of the house and one of them was hurt. I knew that was Chris Breen.

Two of the men had gone in Vinnie Rourke's car and another had taken mine.

They were afraid of my car being linked to Joe Murray. This wasn't working out so bad. There were no definite leads.

When Mrs Mitchell and Niamh came back I said, 'Listen, if there's anyone you want to call and say you're okay, I think you should, but just don't tell them where you are yet.'

She just nodded.

I asked her if she was alright.

I was curious at how calm she was.

'Are you in shock?' I said.

She asked me what I meant.

I said I didn't know and she laughed.

I was beginning to think Mrs Mitchell was a bit of a loolah.

We drove over a bridge and a sign said Boyle, twelve miles.

'My friend, Jeff,' I was telling her, 'always has empty houses, secluded, we can probably stay somewhere like that for a day or two and work things out. Is that okay?'

'Yes,' she said. As if she was annoyed at me. Then Niamh said something about a tree and we smiled.

I was watching the road and thinking about what people were like.

I was tired. There was a house right beside the road. I wanted to live there so I could pull in, sit by the fire and have a few drinks. Eat my dinner and go to bed and in bed, my pretty wife would tell me she wasn't my judge and I'd sleep and sleep and dream until the next thing I'd do which would be an interesting thing.

And no one would bother me.

The day was dark and the rain becoming torrential when we got to Boyle.

Mrs Mitchell waited in the car.

I went over to Jeff's offices beside the memorial and I saw him through the door.

He was talking to a woman who was typing at a computer.

I looked around and went in.

'Jesus,' said Jeff.

I smiled and asked him if he had a minute.

'Come on,' he said, and we went into his office.

'I'm in trouble,' I told him.

'I'm going to be straight with you. I've killed someone and I need somewhere to go.'

'Is this the thing on the radio?' he said.

'It's not my fault,' I told him.

'They're looking for a woman and a kid.'

He was smarter than he looked.

'It's not a kidnap,' I told him, 'They're in the car.' I told him what had happened.

He sat down and didn't look well for a few minutes and then he said, 'Come on.'

I followed him out. He asked his secretary for some keys.

'Wait till you see this place,' he said.

We went out into the rain.

'Get them,' said Jeff, 'We'll take my car and dump that one later.'

And as I ran across to the Fiesta, he shouted, 'It's nice to see you.' I swung around and we were laughing.

I told Mrs Mitchell we'd been sorted out.

Niamh had been sick.

'That's okay, Niamh,' I said, 'It's not our car.'

Jeff pulled alongside and Mrs Mitchell took Niamh into the back.

I introduced everyone.

Jeff said, 'How are you Niamh, chicken, a bit carsick?'

'She's alright now,' said Mrs Mitchell.

'And how are you?' said Jeff.

'I'm okay,' she said.

Then Jeff said, 'It's over now, I promise you'll all be safe.'

Mrs Mitchell said this was the worst rain she'd ever seen, and Jeff asked us if it was raining in Dublin.

I wondered if I was in a car full of fucking loopers.

We drove for about ten miles with the wipers on full tilt.

Jeff was telling us a story about a time his car was stuck in the mud after he'd been drinking at some festival in Galway.

It was one of those stories where everyone ends up covered in mud, pushing the wrong car into a lake.

I closed my eyes and listened to Jeff.

And I could feel Niamh's breath in my ear as she stood between the seats.

I wondered if things were getting better or if Jeff was just one of those people.

'And here we are,' he said.

We turned through a pair of huge gates and drove up a tree-lined avenue.

And in a wide hollow was a house as big as the GPO.

'Be it ever so humble,' said Jeff.

'Look where we're going to stay, Niamh,' said Mrs Mitchell.

Jeff was grinning to save his life.

We went in through high narrow doors.

We were in a tiled hallway.

The door straight ahead lead to a similar back hall and we could see a huge garden which sloped down to the Shannon where it was wide and islands stretched across to a newly planted forest.

We walked around looking for ghosts.

Jeff was talking to us.

But I wasn't listening. I was too busy smelling the air.

The rooms were empty and recently refloored.

The boards gave off an unexpected warmth.

The rain hammered off the windows.

I stood in the darkening ballroom.

Jeff took Mrs Mitchell with Niamh in her arms up to the next floor.

I heard him tell her how surprisingly cheap a place like this was.

I sat with my back to the wall and put my revolver on my lap.

I closed my eyes and listened to the rain and the wind.

I was dreaming about the heart of the countryside beating.

I was in the veins like a sickness and Greta's hands were in my clean hair and we lay just beneath the clouds wondering when the storm would end.

I woke to sunshine blazing across the floor. I was wrapped in a quilt and soft little hands were on my face. Niamh ran across to the windows in her bare feet.

I heard voices. Laughing. Children shouting. My revolver was pressing against my shoulderblade.

I sat up. It was eleven o'clock.

Jeff came in and said, 'You're alive.' Fucking comedian.

He had a flask.

He sat down beside me and I drank a cup of coffee.

He told me he had brought his wife, Marie, and the kids over. Marie and Mrs Mitchell were organising a picnic. This was blowing my mind.

I wanted to know if we were safe.

'I think so,' he said.

He showed me the papers.

People seemed to think it was some sort of fucked-up IRA thing, which suited me fine.

The guards were appealing for information about the cars.

They didn't have any registrations.

They found Mitchell's car in Kinnegad, and they were looking for the Fiesta.

Nobody had seen us yet.

Jeff had it stashed in the garage of a house he was selling which didn't get many viewers.

As long as nothing linked it to me or Murray no one would find us up here in Leitrim, which is where we turned out to be.

Jeff gave me clean clothes and razors and stuff. I showered upstairs in an en-suite bathroom.

Out the window I could see Mrs Mitchell and Marie organising blankets on the lawn.

Everything was on a huge plastic sheet.

Jeff was playing with the kids.

He picked Niamh up and swung her around, chasing the others with her in his arms.

She was in hysterics.

On the blankets Jeff's baby was lying on her belly, rolling onto her back.

I went down.

Marie kissed me and gave me a long hug.

Mrs Mitchell smiled at me.

I sat down and played with the baby.

She squeezed my fingers tightly, even though she was tiny.

I liked the pressure.

There were sandwiches, meat, salad, cake, wine, beer and coffee all on paper plates spread over the blankets.

I smoked one of Marie's Marlboros and had a beer.

I held the baby on my lap and we all laughed at her.

Mrs Mitchell sat beside me and drank Piat d'Or from a paper cup.

She said she hadn't seen Niamh have so much fun in ages.

'They're great kids,' I said.

Marie took the baby from me to change her nappy. Jeff was rounding up the children.

I asked Mrs Mitchell if she'd seen the papers. She said she had and then became upset. I tried to comfort her, but she pulled away from me and said 'Look, you're not my friend, okay?'

I nodded.

We didn't say anything for a minute.

Then she said, 'Sorry.'

And I said, 'No.'

She said she'd made a call.

'To who?' I asked her.

But Marie came back, shouting 'Come on, everybody.'

The kids stuffed themselves.

I was starving too.

I must've ate about a loaf of seafood sandwiches which were Marie's thing.

I drank a few beers, but I really wanted to get Mrs Mitchell on her own and ask her who the fuck she'd called.

So I asked her to come for a walk.

We went down to the river.

THE GOOD THIEF 75

The baby was crying.

'Who did you ring?' I asked her.

She sat on a rock and put her feet in the water.

'Oh that's freezing,' she said, 'I thought it'd be warmer.'

I smacked the back of her head and grabbed her hair.

I told her that if she fucked me around, I'd break every bone in her body.

I'd really lost my temper.

She didn't shout. She didn't make a sound.

I let her go and she said, 'I rang Niamh's father, alright?'

I wanted to know what she was talking about.

'Patrick Mitchell wasn't her father,' she said, 'I had been seeing someone.'

She gave me a story about some teenage sweetheart coming back into her life a year or two after she'd married Mitchell.

She wouldn't sleep with Mitchell and he was going bananas. He was going to move them all to England which is why he was trying to sort the Joe Murray thing out.

But there was no way she was going.

She wanted to be with this man.

But he was a journalist who travelled around a lot and he wasn't ready to settle down and support them.

That's why she was still with Mitchell when he died.

Like so many fucking things.

She needed a roof over her head.

So she'd rung this man in Paris saying what had happened, but that she was safe.

She hadn't told him where she was but he was coming to Ireland.

'You have to believe me,' she said.

I did believe her.

For one thing, it seemed to explain her less than widowly grief.

'You make me sick,' I said. And walked off. She chased me and punched my back.

'What do you mean?' she shouted.

But I knew I hadn't meant her.

I was sorry I'd said it.

She became upset again and this time when I put my arm around her, she cried into my chest.

And I was thinking about Joe Murray on top of Greta.

I told her I was sure it would work out.

'Come on Mrs Mitchell,' I said, 'Let's have a drink.'

She laughed at me calling her Mrs Mitchell and said her name was Anna.

I told her I was sorry for all the shit that had happened. But I was trying to feel sorry and I don't think I really did.

Not that I was glad. I don't mean that at all.

She seemed to cheer up a little bit then and we spent the rest of the afternoon drinking and watching the children.

The baby fell asleep in my arms.

Jeff went down and swam. The kids jumped around on the shore and he splashed them.

The rest of us smoked and chatted occasionally.

At dusk it began to get a bit chilly.

We went inside and sat in the ballroom.

The children were tired and it was time for Jeff to bring his family home.

Marie was saying goodbye to Mrs Mitchell.

I wondered if I should ring Joe Murray.

But Jeff said he'd be back in the morning and we could decide what to do then.

Mrs Mitchell had slept upstairs the night before but she moved her stuff down beside mine.

When Jeff was gone she laid Niamh down in the quilt and we spoke quietly for a while.

Her boyfriend was a freelance writer and she seemed to love him very much. He knew he was Niamh's father, but he'd only seen her three times.

Mr Mitchell had thought Niamh was his.

She had been conceived during a two-week daily sex session at the Mitchell's house while he was at work.

I felt sorry for the poor bastard.

Mrs Mitchell hoped to get out of the country without being involved in any investigation.

We joked for a while about what colour she should dye her hair to avoid being recognised. She wanted to know what I was going to do. I didn't know. I told her I hadn't any commitments or ties.

I sort of wanted to talk about Greta but I didn't know where to begin.

We settled down for the night.

I could feel them lying beside me and when I listened to them breathing it felt like my soul was being bleached.

I woke to the sound of glass breaking.

'What is it?' I heard Mrs Mitchell say.

It was pitch dark.

I took my pistol and told her to stay where she was.

I made my way to the front door.

It was open and the breeze filled the hall.

I couldn't see anyone.

I moved my way back toward the ballroom, feeling for a light switch.

'Mrs Mitchell?' I whispered.

A torch went on and something bounced off my head.

I was very groggy.

I could see that dawn was coming and that there were people in the room.

My hands were cuffed behind me and I had no clothes on.

I was sitting on the floor.

I passed out again.

Then I was slapped.

This time it was brighter.

Vinnie Rourke's friend, Seamus Parker was slapping me.

'Get your fucking hands off me,' I said.

Someone kicked me in the back. I collapsed and I couldn't move.

The feeling came back gradually and I wished it wouldn't.

'Get him up,' someone said.

I was dragged to my feet by Seamus Parker and someone else I didn't know.

Vinnie Rourke stood in front of me and quick as he could, he gave me three digs, two in the stomach and one in the face.

He did it so fast I knew he was showing off.

I took a step backwards but they held me steady.

'Where's Joe Murray?' I asked.

They all started digging me.

I was surprised how weak their punches were.

Maybe it was they were up all night.

I was getting worried about Mrs Mitchell and Niamh. But I didn't want to say anything.

I didn't want to draw attention to them.

I wanted them to be forgotten.

Vinnie Rourke grabbed my bollocks and gave them a good wrench.

It was agony, but it was sort of funny.

I asked him if he was enjoying himself.

He got a bit annoyed.

I said I never knew he was a poof.

That did the job. He let go and told me he'd show me who was a poof.

He kicked my legs so hard I was leaping in Seamus Parker's arms.

Then I was on the floor.

I knew he'd break my neck if he kept kicking me. I was passing out.

I saw Greta and Mrs Mitchell leading me up some stairs in newly painted flats beside a river. There was a war and they were looking after me.

Then I was drenched on the floor.

Vinnie Rourke had poured a bucket of water over me.

My left eye was closing.

I could just see Joe Murray sitting on a chair above me.

Nobody said anything.

I smiled at him and he looked away.

Then he asked me what I thought I was playing at.

I tried to speak and something fell out of my mouth.

I ran my tongue along the gaps in my teeth.

'For fuck's sake,' said Murray.

I managed to say 'How . . . ?'

'How did we find you?' he said, 'Don't be dense. Greta knew where you'd go. You see,' he said, 'she loves me so she told me. How does that make you feel?'

I was disappointed, but something cheered me up. And it was something I knew about and Joe Murray didn't. Greta didn't love anybody. He didn't know her at all.

'What are you grinning at?' he said. 'You little bastard. We looked after your friend. We looked after that fucker.'

I knew he must have found out where we were from Jeff. But Jeff wouldn't have told him simply because he was asked nicely.

'It was like the towering fucking inferno,' he said.

I thought he might be bluffing but I wasn't very hopeful that Jeff and his family were still alive.

I was waiting for him to get on with it and shoot me.

I wondered whose fault this was.

'And I suppose you want to know about flat-chest Mitchell and the sprog,' said Murray and the way he said it told me everything.

When I was out cold, they'd had a party.

Maybe that dream I'd had of her when I was getting that kicking was her soul and she had met me while things were happening to her body. I still like to think that.

Murray was talking.

'Greta did us a favour telling me where you were, and we're going to do something for her. She asked us to let you live.'

I couldn't believe it. She had been thinking about me. She wanted me to be alive.

He went on.

'We've worked something out. In a few hours you'll be arrested here. There'll be evidence the Mitchells were here, but not enough to completely fuck you. Keep your mouth shut, make something up and you'll get accessory, five to ten years we reckon.'

He got up and signalled the others to go.

Then he said, 'Mention me or anybody and we'll kill you. I'm only doing this for Greta. She says I can trust you. And I have to trust her. Don't I? I mean, I'm not young any more. I have to make a commitment.'

I motioned to him with my head and he leaned over me.

'Just don't put it in her arse,' I said.

I don't know if he heard me or not.

He just got up and left.

I lay there throbbing from the kicks and I thought my heart would burst.

Sure enough towards afternoon the guards came.

I was taken to hospital and I wouldn't answer any questions.

I turned off in every interrogation.

I just thought about Greta.

I was wondering what she was doing at the precise moment I was thinking about her.

Funny, I always imagined her having a bath.

Eventually I confessed to a kidnapping.

But I said I was only the driver.

I didn't know that Mitchell had been killed and I was waiting for a ransom for us to release Mrs Mitchell.

The other kidnappers had double-crossed me and beat me. I didn't know their real names. I thought they were English.

The guards saw this for the rubbish it was, but it was all they had.

They'd found me tied up and in bits. They knew I couldn't have done that to myself, and although they linked me to Jeff, whoever had done the arson job on his house had made it look accidental enough.

My army record was good, I'd never been arrested before.

Mrs Mitchell and Niamh were never found.

No bodies, no murder charge.

At my trial I think everyone thought I was some sort of idiot.

But fuck that. I got ten years.

I didn't think very much for the next few weeks.

I just went along day by day.

I felt sad all of the time.

But I'm not sure what I felt sad about.

And I know how stupid that sounds.

Then the sad feeling went and I just thought about Greta.

I wanted to kill Joe Murray and Vinnie Rourke.

It was the only reason I wanted to get out.

And after that I didn't really feel anything.

Sometimes I woke up thinking Niamh's hands were on my face and I would wish that everyone was still alive. But these were more feelings than thoughts.

They ran through me and they were spilt milk.

I knew nothing good could come out of what had happened because of everybody's stupidity.

Then one day someone was put in my cell with me.

His name was Tom Vander.

He was twenty, a burglar.

We didn't speak much to begin with, which isn't to say we weren't friendly.

He didn't make many friends and pretty much stayed on his own.

Then one evening we just sort of got talking.

He had started breaking into houses around where he lived, in Clontarf, about a year before.

He liked the feeling of being in someone else's house with all their private things.

Sometimes, he'd even take a bath.

I thought this was very funny.

He never stole much. Just cash, if he found it, but he never looked very hard.

The odd time he'd watch their videos or look through their books.

He might sound a bit spacey, but he was alright. He was a good laugh.

We never bothered each other if one of us wasn't in a talky mood.

We were happy enough reading or just listening to tapes.

One night I told him all about Mrs Mitchell and Niamh and everything that had happened.

He didn't say anything about it and I was glad he didn't. He just knew it was something you couldn't say anything about.

I told him about Greta and he told me about his girlfriends and how he'd had sex up a tree one time.

That night I heard him wanking in the bunk above me and I wanked too.

We wanked a lot after that. We knew when either of us were doing it and we made up filthy stories while we did it.

This usually ended in hysterics.

Then one blazing summer's day, Tom was released.

I knew he was getting out but I hadn't thought about it much. He was delighted and I was too. But then I felt crap because one day he was there and the next he wasn't and I couldn't talk to him any more.

He went to England.

He wrote for a while and then he got engaged and didn't write after that.

My own company wasn't good enough for me any more.

And it wasn't that I wanted to be entertained or anything, I wanted to make someone else happy.

I wanted to be there when they needed me.

I don't live in Ireland any more.

I drink too much and I hardly go out.

I sometimes wonder about the type of person I am, but not for long.

I'm no good.

Sometimes when the clouds are low and I look out the window with one eye on the pillow I still think about Mrs Mitchell and Niamh and Jeff's family.

And I think about Greta and the time I saw her last year.

It was a filthy wet day and she got out of a big car with a man twice her age.

I thought about walking up to her but I was trying to get out of the rain.

THIS LIME TREE BOWER

For Jack McPherson

        A delight
Comes sudden on my heart, and I am glad
As I myself were there! Nor in this bower,
This little lime tree bower, have I not marked
Much that has soothed me.

 . . . No sound is dissonant which tells of life.

Samuel Taylor Coleridge,
'This Lime Tree Bower My Prison',
1797

This Lime Tree Bower was first performed as an Íomhá Ildánach/Fly by Night co-production at the Crypt Arts Centre, Dublin, on 26 September 1995, with the following cast:

JOE   Ian Cregg
RAY   Conor Mullen
FRANK   Niall Shanahan

Director   Conor McPherson
Designer   John O'Brien and Conor McPherson
Lighting Designer   Paul Winters
Producer   Philip Gray

The play was subsequently performed at the Bush Theatre, London, from 3 July 1996, with the same cast and production team, with the exception of the lighting, which was designed by Paul Russell.

Characters

JOE, *seventeen*

RAY, *early thirties*

FRANK, *twenties*

All remain on stage throughout, and are certainly aware of each other.

JOE

Damien came to our school halfway through the term.

He was different from everybody else there.

Even his uniform made him look good.

He had a long fringe, bleached, and he had a tan.

He always smoked and he never went home at lunchtime. I found out that he didn't live too far away, and he probably had the coolest bike in the whole school, but at lunchtime, he hung around.

I started smoking too, so I could talk to him at little break behind the religion room. It was completely fucking disgusting.

You were supposed to be dying for a pull and about nine blokes would be sharing a fag. By the time it came around to you it was just a soaking-wet filter.

And you had to drag on it like you'd die without it.

But I got to talk to Damien.

I pretended my bike was broken and I brought sandwiches in so I could hang around at big break.

The lads who stayed in all got chips in the Chinese, which I wouldn't get because of what my dad had told me about them.

The lads who ate them all had huge spots, except for Damien.

He was only in three of my classes, and one of them was civics, which we only had once a week, but I could never wait for him to come in.

He was never on time and in the mornings if I was in a room where I could see the driveway, I'd watch for him.

I never once saw him arrive but he'd always be there.

That's the way it is when you like someone – you can never see them.

I tried to tell Frank, my brother, about Damien, but he called me a poofter and told me to go asleep.

Frank was five years older than me and worked with my dad in our chipper.

I only worked there during the holidays.

It was never busy till then.

No one comes to the seaside when it's raining, which is weird, because that's when I liked it best.

When it was all grey and the waves splashed up on the road is when I liked it.

Those sort of days my dad had a pint in Reynolds and read the paper.

I used to go in and sit with him sometimes.

Like on a Saturday.

He told me once that drinking is no way for a man to sort anything out, but that he only found out too late.

I told him not to be silly.

Frank said that Dad's problems were none of his doing.

He owed a big loan to Simple Simon McCurdie.

Simple Simon was a councillor and owned the bookies down the street.

Frank said he was far from simple.

We didn't know how he got the name.

But he had it.

And that's what we called him.

I'm quite shrewd and I know how to do things in ways that don't look really obvious.

That's how I made friends with Damien.

We'd just find ourselves standing together.

I saw what bands he had, written on his bag and on his journal.

I let on to like them too.

And because he'd come halfway through the term, he didn't know anyone.

Sometimes I'd pretend not to see him and he'd still come over to me.

So I knew he liked me.

He was kicked out of his last school for being on the mitch and smoking in PE.

He had told a teacher to fuck off and she had just got out of hospital or something and she started crying.

He was lucky to get into our school because not many places would take someone like that.

But then, my school was a dump.

Someone who lived near Damien said he hadn't been expelled at all.

He had left because he was always being slagged for only having one ball.

But somebody always says something.

I reckon our school had pity on him because he needed somewhere to do his leaving.

He told me about the girls he'd shagged and how he could always tell when someone was a virgin.

I blushed so badly that I had to pretend to blow my nose so he wouldn't see.

He asked me to bonk off school one Friday.

I'd never done it before and I knew I'd be killed.

But Damien said he was an expert forger and he'd give me a brilliant note.

We arranged to meet at the roundabout on the dual carriageway at nine o' clock.

I was waiting for ages.

I thought everyone was looking at me.

And I knew that Miss Brosnan, our biology teacher, used to drive around looking for boys on the mitch when she had a free class. She had huge tits and we used to pretend there was something wrong with the microscopes so she'd bend over to have a look.

I was imagining her catching me on the mitch and making me fuck her as a punishment.

I was too scared to go off on my own and I was going to go in late and get detention.

But then Damien showed up.

He didn't even have his uniform on.

We cycled around the suburbs and stayed off the main roads. It felt brilliant.

All the people were at work.

I saw women wheeling kids out of the supermarket and I thought about me being with my mum when I was like that.

We went into the park.

It was dark under the trees and we scrambled up and down the hills.

Then it was nearly one and we sat down and ate our lunch.

We could see two girls from Holy Faith going through the park to the shops.

Damien knew them.

They were gorgeous and I felt like an ugly bollocks.

One was blonde and one was dark like she was foreign.

Damien made them laugh about people they knew and I didn't.

I wanted to hold their hands and stroll through town with lots of money.

They didn't say anything to me, but they looked at me like if I was with Damien, there must be something good about me.

But they couldn't see what.

I sucked in my cheeks and pretended not to be interested.

I fiddled with my gears and broke them.

When the girls were gone we sat under the trees where we could see the beach.

My stomach was all tingly.

Damien said the blonde one, Tara, would ride anybody. She had had it off with most of his friends and Damien had screwed her when he was fourteen.

I asked him how it had happened and I immediately felt like a cretin.

Damien just said, 'Got a boner. Stuck it in.'

Then he went off for a piss and he was gone for ages.

I had to go looking for him, but when I found him I let on I was just cycling around.

He told me his dad was living with some woman and that his mum had had him when she was sixteen.

He started saying how cool she was and we should go home and see her.

I told him school wasn't over yet.

He said his mum couldn't give two shits.

They lived out by the Old Strand Road where all the Protestants lived.

The house had a long front garden with high trees. There was a boat in the drive but Damien said it didn't go.

There was a lawnmower in the hall and the carpet was filthy.

There was a spicy smell.

We had toast and peanut butter and watched MTV. There were bottles everywhere.

I looked out the back. The garden was lower than the front.

Then Damien's mum came in.

She was small and she had jeans and runners.

She didn't look like any of the mums I knew.

She had too much make-up and I could see she had no bra.

She ignored me and asked Damien why he wasn't in school.

A man came in behind her and went straight out the back.

A huge dog ran after him and the man took off his shirt.

I watched him run around with the dog and then he jumped into a muddy pond at the bottom of the garden, with his pants still on.

Damien shouted at his mum not to give him a hard time – she was doing his head in.

She stopped giving out then and gave him a kiss.

He put his hand on her arse and she was looking at me and giggling.

I was sort of laughing too, but I didn't think it was funny.

I was being false.

I went out pretending I really had a thing for dogs. The dog didn't come near me though. I sat in the kitchen door and watched the man.

He was putting his head under the water and coming up saying, 'Jeeesus, Jeeesus Christ!'

Damien came out and I asked him who the man was. But Damien didn't know. He must've been a friend of his mum's he thought.

The man shouted at us not to mind him because he was a bit pissed.

Damien's mum came out and said, 'Peter, what are you doing?'

Then she laughed and ran down to the pond.

I went home then.

Damien wanted me to stay but I felt funny.

Then I was too early.

I had to wait outside Simple Simon's bookies for a quarter of an hour till school was over.

Simple Simon saw me and came out.

He was really fat and he scared the shit out of me.

He leaned against the door frame all chummy with his arms folded.

He didn't say anything for a minute, like we were really used to each other.

Then he asked how Dad was.

I said alright, thanks.

'Good, good,' he said.

He was always saying that, 'Good, good,' like it was some catchphrase the audience loved.

Then he showed what a bollocks he was and asked me if I was on the mitch.

I said no.

And he said, 'Why are you hanging around here then? What are you waiting for?'

He said it like he was going to slap me but then he broke his shit laughing.

I gave him the false laugh I was getting good at and cycled off.

He told me to say hello to Frank for him.

Frank said Simple Simon was a fucking leech when I told him.

He was wiping tables and filling ketchup in our sit-down part.

Dad was out the back with his head under the bonnet. He asked me how school was.

I shouted fine and ran upstairs.

I lay in my room and wanked and thought about the girls in the park, and they loved me because there had been a nuclear blast and there was no one left in the world.

Only us. They had to share me.

They had to take turns.

It was just to have a good wank.

Because the girl I really fancied was Deborah Something.

She lived down the road and I'd only ever seen her from the side.

My sister Carmel was in the shower because her boyfriend Ray was coming.

He had a great car because he had this really good job lecturing in a college.

He gave out about it a lot.

He said the thickest people he ever met were all in third-level institutions.

One time he showed us a journal called *Ethics* because he had an article in it.

I couldn't grasp what it was about but you could see he was clever.

Him and Dad and Frank would sit up drinking whiskey and watching the late news programmes. Then they'd give out about the politicians and the reporters and anybody they saw.

They slagged what everybody said and the way everybody looked.

That was the way it was.

I don't know what Ray was doing hanging around with my sister.

Maybe he wasn't clever all the time.

Or just blind.

RAY

I woke up on a cold October morning in bed with one of my students.

What was her name? I can't remember.

I got up, put on my Dunnes Stores' jumper and underpants.

I always wore khaki trousers in those days.

It was kind of . . . a thing with me.

The room was freezing.

All the usual shit. Paper light shade, Stone Roses poster, a load of fucking awful books I'd never read and all the empty bottles of wine she'd drunk over the last God knows.

Her hair was sticking out over the quilt.

She was a bit of a chubby yoke, and for a minute I felt like hopping back in and giving her one. From behind.

But it was a passing yen and I had a lecture to give at twelve.

I felt like absolute shite.

I was putting on weight and I needed a haircut and a shave.

Had to wash my face in cold water.

Didn't bother waking her up. Fuck her.

I went down and got into the Saab.

And just my luck, it was always a bitch to start on a cold morning.

By the time I got it going she was looking out the window.

I pretended not to see.

She turned away quickly and I just knew she was going to leg it down to the garden. But by that time I was long gone.

Going down the dual carriageway, me, Pat, Elaine and the fucking Morning Crew, and my hangover was coming into its own.

I'd started the afternoon before with a quiet pint in the student bar.

Now I always drank in the student bar because I hate academics.

I don't really like students either, but there you are.

Well a few of them joined me and they're buying me pints.

And what do you know? It's nine o'clock and there's a disco on.

Girl from my third-year utilitarianism group in a leather mini and I'm up dancing.

One of the kids . . .

And I was thinking about these sort of German bohemians in Hamburg trying to understand The Beatles. Like these kids trying to work me out. See what makes me tick.

We paused for cocktails. There was a tequila promotion on. Few of them and I'm back up again.

For a minute, I forgot who I was.

And then I remembered and I spun round and round like a kid and it was all coming back and then I puked right there in front of everybody.

People slipped in it, the place was mayhem.

The lights came on and for some reason I offered to pay for the mess.

Then it was time for lifts home.

Out into the wind and drizzle.

There's five of them in the fucking car.

I was annoyed now.

Someone put on a tape. It was a comedy thing which wasn't remotely fucking funny.

First stop, Blackrock. Two girls get out.

They're talking philosophy in the back of the car. This fucking kid with long manky hair is nearly screaming some stupid theory about Karl Popper so I'll hear him and . . . remember him for ever, or give him a job or something.

And everyone else is going, 'Just shut the fuck up, Vyvyan.' Back across the dualer into Goatstown.

Then it's just me and her.

She lives in Mount Merrion.

She invites me in.

I check she doesn't live with her parents – happened to me before when I was working as a tutor in England.

I was banging this first-year in the morning and her mother came in to wake her for college. You can't take anything for granted.

It was cool. So in we go. I crash on her bed. I wake up. Three in the morning. I roll over. We do it.

It was shite.

Anyway, into college.

I parked behind the bar and thought about how long it had been since I was in there. Eleven and a half. Eleven and a fucking half hours.

I had to give a twelve o' clock in Theatre O. I'd enough time to get a cure.

I sat in the filthy bar and laid into about four gin and tonics because I'd heard somewhere that they were supposed to be good for a hangover.

But that's probably bullshit too.

Nothing works except getting pissed again.

It's a dreadful fucking world, isn't it?

I made up my mind not to feel guilty.

Carmel could never find out. Our lives were too separate.

Of course, this was something I could lose my job over. But it was just the state I was in I couldn't give a fuck.

I waffled my way through the lecture.

There were only about twenty there.

The rest probably all had hangovers.

I fucking turned up. Ingrates.

Up in my office the wind was howling.

I watched the trees blowing.

I went and had a huge shite.

Then I put my head on my desk and snoozed.

I dreamt I'd organised a recording of *Under Milk Wood* in my flat.

John Rawls came down from the mountains and his wife was choosy about what she ate.

I woke with someone knocking at the door. I looked at my watch.

Three o'clock. Twelve hours since I'd rolled over.

And there she was at the door.

She came in and started crying.

I gave her a tissue. Told her it wasn't a big deal.

I joked with her and she cheered up.

With some girls it's just about pushing the right buttons, isn't it?

We drove to a quiet pub out near Rathfarnham.

After a few drinks and something to eat, I said, 'Friends again?' She smiled.

Yeah, we'd been stupid. We admitted it.

But we were adults.

We could put it behind us.

There was nothing to worry about.

Inside, I was seething.

Thinking about what a stupid fat bitch she was. Doing this on me.

Her little moment of glory.

I couldn't breathe. My stomach was full of acid.

I nearly lost my temper but I kept my cool.

At seven I gave her a lift into town.

She was going to The Stag's Head.

All I needed now was for her to have a bun in the oven. That'd be just fucking great.

It was time to see Carmel.

Carmel had these . . . country virtues.

That whole Greek idea of the good life.

The life lived well.

I fancied a few beers with her brother, Frank. Shoot the shit for a while and then later, when everyone was in bed me and Carmel would go up to her room.

You see, I was sort of in the middle of an experiment in those days.

I wanted to have a really vigorous fuck and break the condom.

Driving down the Malahide Road, I touched ninety twice.

Life in the old girl yet.

FRANK

I remember that Friday.

The weather had been rotten all week.

It was freezing when I woke up.

Dad was out the back, messing with the car. I told him to leave it and let Ray have a look. Ray knew a few bits and pieces about engines and that. He was a great driver. And he usually called over to see Carmel on a Friday.

Dad was always fucking around with the engine. It was an old Peugeot 205.

He never went anywhere in it since Mum died. He didn't have the will.

He didn't have any reason to go in it.

And this made him think there was something wrong with it.

People always blame something, don't they?

I normally got up about eleven.

We opened at twelve on the dot.

I had just sort of drifted into working with Dad. He couldn't afford to pay me a fortune.

But I was living at home.

I had no overheads.

It was boring but it was better than nothing.

Because there's nothing worse than a seaside town in the winter when there's nobody about.

We had our regulars at lunchtime.

They'd come around from the bank and the shopping centre.

That was a little belt for about an hour.

Then about four, people would send their kids in for the tea.

Friday teatime was always good.

Sevenish, it'd slack off till the pubs closed.

We stayed open till one at the weekends, half eleven, twelve on weekdays.

It was usually just me and Dad.

But sometimes Joe would drag his heels around, 'working'.

But he hated it.

Carmel was too busy to help.

She was being trained as something at the new financial services centre in the city, which sounded good. But she never said much about it, so it was probably a load of shite.

I had a couple of nights off, mid-week, when Dad just did takeaways.

There was nothing to do, except sit in Reynolds bar and listen to the old lads going on about when the INLA split from the officials and all that sort of thing they could get into a fight about.

If Simple Simon McCurdie was there, they'd use him as a sort of umpire.

He'd sit at the bar with a bottle of Blackbush and nod at them wisely whenever anyone mentioned Seamus Costello or Cathal Goulding.

I'd head back to give Dad a hand about eleven.

First thing in the morning, I'd turn on the fat and the telly.

Anne and Nick were my favourite, Nick always seemed to be taking the piss out of Anne. I'd have it on in the back and just be listening to it while I worked.

I did the chopping and cleaning while Dad did the batter.

He'd lost a lot of weight over the last while and he was drinking too much but he was cheerful and everybody liked him.

Since I'd been sort of full-time we'd been getting on great.

He had all these stories he kept telling over and over with little exaggerations getting worse all the time. But I never got tired of them.

Just before twelve, he'd have his first small one of the day.

He said it helped his blood flow more easily.

I'd gotten used to it, but sometimes I felt it was a bit early.

Because he'd have a couple with his dinner, and from teatime on, he'd sort of be topping it up.

That Friday I opened up a bit late.

People came in from about half.

I took orders in our sit-down part and Dad would put them on the counter.

I was like a waiter and the people knew me. I'd chat with them. Have a laugh.

Mostly though, people took their food away.

Then, about two, Simple Simon came in with his nephew, Charlie Dunne.

I was pissed off because they went into the sit-down part.

Dad wiped his hands and told me to get behind the counter. And he went to deal with Simple Simon himself.

Simon was a local councillor and had the only bookies in the town.

Dad owed him a couple of grand.

He borrowed it when Mum died.

He should've gone to a bank or the credit union, but he'd owed Simple Simon money before from stupid bets.

And Simon used to let him off.

He knew Dad wasn't going anywhere and if it came down to it, Dad could always give him a share in the chipper.

So Dad, like a fucking gobshite, thought he had a special relationship.

As if friends could never let money upset them.

Well he was learning the hard way because now Simon was calling in the loan.

And it was killing my dad.

I knew one of the reasons he kept tinkering with the car was because he was wondering if anyone would buy it.

But it could only go for parts and he'd be lucky to get two hundred for it. Like very lucky.

And I hated Simple Simon because he knew exactly what he was doing.

It would break your heart to see Dad trying to butter him up and Simon playing the patient generous old uncle.

He was a miserable cunt.

He wanted a smoked cod and chips and his nephew Charlie wanted a quarter pounder with cheese, two battered sausages, chips, and bread and butter.

Simple Simon used to always introduce Charlie as 'my sister's boy'.

'This is Charlie, my sister's boy,' he used to say. I think he said it to reassure people that Charlie wasn't some sort of scientific experiment.

His head was too big but his face was tiny.

And his arms were too long so he always had his hands in his trouser pockets like he couldn't stop playing with himself.

I wanted to spit in their tea but Dad would've killed me.

When I brought their stuff over Simon was acting like me and him shared some big secret that we both found funny.

He was always offering me a job.

He told me his fingers were in lots of pies and there were fewer and fewer ways out of this town.

I pretended I'd love to take him up but told him that my dad needed me.

He told me to think about it and he squeezed my elbow.

Charlie asked me for 'red sauce', which the rest of us know as ketchup and it gave me an excuse to fuck off.

They stayed for ages.

Simon read the *Independent.*

And Charlie didn't do anything.

He just sat there with his hands in his pockets.

And he seemed perfectly fucking content just to do that.

It scared the shit out of me.

It must have been getting on for three when they left.

Dad ran out after them to say goodbye, wiping his hands like Simple Simon was going to check them.

Charlie nodded at me. I was fascinated by the size of his head so I nodded back.

To make him do it again.

Of course, they didn't pay and my dad shot me a look that said he didn't want to hear any shit from me.

And I think it was then that the mad plan started to form.

And once it started, I couldn't stop.

There was a big bloke with a beard used to come into Reynolds the odd time.

The old lads always bought him drinks, but he wouldn't chat much.

Most people steered clear of him.

He'd only ever come in the chipper about nine, when it was quiet. And he was usually there on a Friday.

If it was me serving him, I'd have a cup of tea while he ate. We'd talk shit mostly, and I wouldn't say I knew him particularly well. But I had heard a few different stories about him, in Reynolds.

Fran Ferris said he was a gunman from the north who'd escaped and they couldn't extradite him. Shamey Devereaux said he was an armed robber out on parole trying to stay out of trouble.

This could well have been a load of bollocks and he might have worked in Super Value – but I have to admit, there was something about him. And as far as I knew, Reynolds was the only place would even serve him.

That night, Ray called about eight and he was upstairs with Carmel and Dad.

Joe was in our room and it was a fairly safe bet he was having a wank.

Everyone thought he was great.

He was always studying.

The bloke with the beard came in about half nine.

He asked me for a fresh cod and chips.

I was wondering what type of person he was.

The only thing I definitely knew about him was that he liked fish.

He was reading his paper when I brought it over to him.

The place was empty.

My heart was banging away like the Peugeot.

I sat down opposite him.

'Listen,' I said, 'I may be barking up the wrong tree completely, but I want to ask you something.'

He kept on eating and didn't look at me.

'What is it?' he said.

'I need a gun.'

He took a sup of tea and then he put it down and said, 'What do you want it for?'

I ate one of his chips.

JOE

I spent the evening with Fergus and Noel.

We were mates since being kids.

They called for me and we had nowhere to go.

We went down to the rocks where the shipwreck was. The tide was out and we could see most of it.

We were never allowed to swim out near it because a boy got stuck in it one time and died. But that was back in the seventies and none of us knew him.

The story was that the ship was carrying guns for the IRA in 1920 or something and the captain was an English fellow who had fallen in love with a girl in the town.

And she was in the womens' IRA.

And she got him to bring the guns over in the night. But she was supposed to marry some farmer further up the coast. And he had found out and and he tipped off the Black and Tans. So they arrested the girl in her house and captured the IRA men who were going down the beach to get the guns.

But the girl knocked over an oil lamp in the house and there was a huge fire.

This warned the captain of the boat and he scuttled it.

He was drowned and because a British soldier died in the fire the girl was hung.

That was the story the old lads in Reynolds used to say about it.

But Frank told me the boat belonged to a fisherman called Vinty Duggan who crashed it after drinking a bottle of Powers.

It was hard to know who to believe.

The town was full of spoofers.

Dad said he wouldn't get involved in the dispute because he was from Italy and it was none of his business.

He said that Irish people would rather make something up and if that's what they liked to do, then he had no problem.

When I told him he was forgetting I was Irish, he just told me to believe what I liked.

Or better still, make up my own spoof about the boat.

But I wasn't really bothered. I just liked looking at it. Lots of things could have been true, who knows?

Fergus and Noel were skulling rocks at the boat and I was having a piss in the sea and I saw the girl I fancied, Deborah Something, up on the promenade.

She was walking along with some bloke.

I felt shit.

We went down to the amusements.

There was only one game I really liked.

It was an old one with a big rifle and you shot at targets that went back into the distance. Even though they were just a few feet away. They just got smaller.

It was only 10p still, because no one ever played it.

When I got home the chipper was closed.

Frank and Carmel and Ray and Dad were watching some film with lawyers and rain.

But only Carmel was really watching it.

The men were drinking and chatting.

I said goodnight and had a shower.

There were clean sheets on my bed and on Frank's. I looked at Frank's books.

He had lots of thrillers and westerns.

I liked his books because the sentences were always short.

The writers gave you the facts.

In school we did books where nobody said what they meant and you had to work out what everybody wanted.

I picked out a book with a black and silver cover.

I always read what the newspapers had said about the book.

Things like, 'You won't find better pace anywhere,' *Chicago Tribune*.

Or, 'I couldn't put it down. The quickfire dialogue and action set-pieces make this a winner,' *Los Angeles Times*.

These books knew how to be read.

They usually started with somebody looking at their watch.

'Jack Brannigan looked at his watch and quietly cursed . . . ' That type of thing.

They also had good sex bits.

Girls whose nipples went as hard as peach stones and their soft skin became covered in goosebumps.

The blokes all had big mickeys and they came quickly the first time.

The next was slow and leisurely.

I read fifty pages of this book.

The ex-cop was a drunk, but he was trying to stay sober.

He was looking for the daughter of a drug dealer who'd been kidnapped.

He knew the city.

But it was changing.

It was summer.

I went under the covers and curled up in the clean sheets.

I was an ex-cop. But I had good in me.

Justice. That kid I shot was an accident.

I woke up when Frank came in.

He was chuckling. I could smell the drink.

I liked Frank, I wanted to be like him.

'Hey Frank,' I said.

'What's the story, Joe?' he asked me.

He was always asking me what the story was. It was three in the morning.

I asked him if he was going to bed.

He just kept laughing.

He told me to go asleep. But I turned on the light. I wouldn't leave him alone till I knew what he was laughing at.

He told me he was going to hold up Simple Simon's bookies.

I asked him when. He said Monday.

And I just thought he was really pissed.

I lay down and I thought about Damien.

I wished it was Monday so I could see him.

I wanted to talk to him about something we were both interested in.

But I couldn't think what that was.

RAY

During the weekend, I drove around with Carmel. The weather picked up and we played tapes. That sort of thing.

I sometimes felt a bit guilty.

Carmel beside me in a light print dress and my mind wandering into different beds.

We stopped for lunch in Longford.

I watched Carmel talking.

She was intelligent.

Probably even more intelligent than me.

But I was together and worldly and she was innocent and trusting.

She had that nobility some people have about them. This showed me what I was and I thought it was a good thing our souls don't have smells.

Because mine would stink.

But at the same time I was proud.

I was getting away with it.

We decided to keep going for Galway and spend the night.

I liked it when a Galway station came on the radio. It was like coming to a new place where you knew nothing about the community. Where they were all used to this radio station I'd never heard.

Do you know what I mean?

No? Fine.

We went to the Great Southern.

I checked in while Carmel rang home.

That hotel smell.

Dinner was from seven.

We went to our room. Thick carpet and a big bed. We swam in the deserted pool.

The chlorine in the air when we got dressed.

We had a few pints in the plush bar and made our way leisurely for a late meal.

If Carmel was unaccustomed to luxury, she didn't show it. She had assurance.

Which annoyed the fuck out of me.

We had a few more drinks. And we were too tired or too full to fuck.

And if you stay in a hotel, you've got to fuck.

So I made a point of waking up early.

We drove home Sunday.

I was refreshed and content.

After dropping Carmel off I went for a few beers with Tony Reagan, our professor.

The famous philosopher, Wolfgang Konigsberg, was visiting our department that week.

He was only giving three lectures.

The department had agreed to this but I wanted the chance of a question-and-answer session where we could discuss his ideas. I knew I could have this guy on the ropes if I had the opportunity to press him, not that I was particularly interested in his area.

Tony said we could talk about it, next day, at the Monday morning staff meeting.

That night I slept the sleep of the just and righteous and all that kind of shit.

The next morning I sat in my office looking at all my beautiful books.

Sometimes I'd go to the library late at night and just sit in between the shelves. Breathing in all those years of useless discussion.

I was working on a book I knew no one was going to read.

What would be the point?

My office was on a corner of the highest part of the college.

This tickled Tony Reagan no end.

He said that the philosophy department was near heaven so that when the questions became too unbearable we could lean out the window and ask God.

Poor Tony was a terrible gobshite.

I sorted out two lectures I wasn't looking forward to giving that afternoon and I went to the staff meeting.

Tony Reagan always wanted to please everyone.

The rationalists, the empiricists, me.

This was a pity because we were just a bunch of selfish children and it wasn't worth it.

He should have just treated us like shit and told us to get on with the philosophy.

But there you are.

The first argument was about who should pick Konigsberg up from the airport.

This took about half an hour.

Trish Meehan was the acknowledged expert on his work, but she was relatively new and Reagan wanted someone who'd represent the department better.

This turned into a squabble.

In the end, six of us were to be at the airport in three cars.

This was lunacy but I kept my mouth shut.

I was waiting for the big picture.

I knew I could fuck Konigsberg up.

Trish Meehan objected to him having to get involved in a discussion, because he was nearly ninety and would already be exhausted from his lectures.

But she was just being a contrary bollocks because she knew no one would touch her with a ten-foot pole. She was taking it out on the world.

I ranted on and on about how undemocratic this was, not to mention the importance of discussion to the progress of ideas, blah blah de blah blah.

Well I might as well have hopped up on the table and taken a dump for all the good it did.

They won, I lost and I fucking hate losing.

The only thing I could salvage was the satisfaction of making Tony Reagan feel bad by pretending to be really upset.

I got up, threw everything into my briefcase, and said I didn't see the point in continuing the pursuit of truth and knowledge in these conditions and some other swine could corrupt the kids in my lectures that afternoon, because I certainly wouldn't.

I gave Trish Meehan the finger on the sly, and I stormed out, slamming the door.

Half day.

Lovely.

FRANK

I had never held one before and I was surprised at how heavy it was.

The barrel had been sawn in half and the wood in the stock was chipped and cracked.

He didn't give me any cartridges.

I asked him when he wanted it back but he just smiled and told me to get rid of it when I was finished.

He was going away and he told me to wish him luck. I did and off he went.

We weren't open yet.

I sat there with the bag at a table.

I thought I was going to have a heart attack. But I felt brilliant at the same time. It was like I could hear and see everything very clearly.

Like I could solve anything by thinking.

It was a feeling of power.

I put the gun upstairs and got on with my work.

Dad joked with me.

He wanted to know if I'd been drinking, I was in that good a mood.

But he was the one who'd had a drink.

He was under so much pressure.

His face was grey.

I hated looking at him in daylight.

His skin hung around him like a coat on a hook.

I thought the fucking eejit was great.

I was going to do something for him.

I waited till things eased off about half two. Dad was reading the paper.

I went upstairs and got my stuff.

I had cut eye-holes in one of Joe's bobble hats. I'd cut the bobble off as well.

I was going to ask him if I could borrow one, but he was in a funny mood.

I had an old Parka jacket and a pair of tracksuit bottoms.

I put the hat on and shoved the shotgun down my pants.

Then I ran down and out the back.

Dad never saw me.

I went across the yard and checked the street. No one about.

I went left down to the seafront and right past the few houses before Simple Simon's.

The street was deserted.

I pulled Joe's hat down over my face and I yanked the gun out.

I took a few deep breaths and walked straight in.

No one noticed me at first.

Charlie was sitting on a stool watching the TV.

Tim Byrne, one of the clerks, was reading the *Irish Independent* and picking his nose.

Two auldfellas were filling out a docket with a stubby pencil.

And the man himself, Simple Simon McFucking Bollocks, walked out from behind the counter with a cup of tea.

'Alright,' I said.

Simon dropped his cup and Charlie fell off the stool.

Tim Byrne put his hands up and the two auldfellas started arguing about the second horse in a treble.

It was easier than I thought it was going to be.

I got everyone to lie on the floor of the shop, then I locked the door.

I told Simple Simon to give me every penny in the place.

He said it wasn't much and it wouldn't be worth my while.

He kept calling me 'son'.

I pulled him up and stuck the gun between his legs.

He went white and did a shit in his pants.

I was smiling behind the hat.

He was telling me to take it easy.

I let him go and he sort of waddled behind the counter.

I jumped up on it so I could watch him and keep an eye on the others.

He pulled about thirty quid out of the till and I took it.

Then I said, 'And the safe.' I didn't even know if he had a safe.

But sure enough, he nearly started to cry and went towards the office.

'Leave the door open,' I told him.

He was kneeling on the floor.

Charlie was glaring up at me with his little piggy eyes.

I was terrified of him. But he just lay there.

Then Simon came back out with two big envelopes.

I leapt off the counter and stuck them in my pockets.

Then I told Simon to take his clothes off.

Naturally, he refused.

But I stuck the gun under his chin and he slowly unbuttoned his pants.

He was shaking so much I thought he was going to have a fit.

I nearly felt sorry for him, standing there with his tits like a girl.

I took him by the hair and we went to the door. I undid the latch and made sure there was no one around.

I waited for a car to turn the corner at Reynolds and I pulled Simon out with me and slammed the door behind us.

I could hear him thumping and shouting to be let back in. And I was around the corner like a shot.

I ran through the yard at the back of the bookies and over to the wall that adjoins the lane. There was a bin and I used it to get up and grab the top of the wall.

And then I nearly collapsed when I heard someone shouting.

Charlie was running towards me.

I fucked the gun over the wall and threw my leg up.

I caught my heel at the top and heaved myself over. The ground was lower on the far side and I fell in a heap.

I could hear Charlie getting up on the bin. I shoved the gun into my pants and started running down the lane.

I pulled Joe's hat off and the gun slipped down my leg. I grabbed it and limped past the back of Creevan's butchers.

I got out on to Main Street and headed for Super Value.

I had to get in somewhere before Charlie came out of the lane.

I could have gone into Mary Kennedy's pub but I never drank there and they'd have been talking about the time I came in for years.

It was too suspicious.

I was trying to walk normally and breathe slowly. Nobody paid me any heed.

But Super Value was too far away.

I was going to be caught.

And then Ray pulled over and gave me a lift.

Interval.

JOE

That Sunday and Monday have to have been the two weirdest days of my life.

Frank didn't say anything about what he'd told me on Friday night, and to tell you the truth I'd forgotten about it.

I thought he was drunk.

Sunday started off normal enough.

Carmel was away with Ray, and Dad and Frank did the dinner.

They'd sort of taken over Mam's jobs about four years before, when she got really sick.

At the time I could remember her dinners and I knew that the new ones were different.

But now I couldn't remember.

I couldn't go to see her much.

I just couldn't.

One time she didn't know who I was and she got a fright when Dad told her.

She was roaring crying.

It was sick. I couldn't stand it.

I was glad when she died.

I had gotten used to her not being at home.

I didn't want to waste time getting upset. It wasn't my fault.

I didn't talk about her and I didn't like thinking about her. It scared me.

And that was all there was to it.

So anyway, after dinner on Sunday I was watching a brutal film and I was going to go up to my room, when the phone rang.

It was Damien.

There was a tickle in my stomach.

He wanted to know if I was going to Shadows.

It was a disco out near the dual carriageway.

Behind the Ancient Mariner bar.

I'd never been there and I knew my dad wouldn't let me go.

The Mariner was called the 'Bucket of Blood' because of all the fights and a barman had lost a finger once, trying to kick someone out.

Dad said it was full of gobshites and knackers.

Frank said that Shadows was crap and that the bouncers spent the whole night kicking people out, because they didn't refuse anyone. To get their money.

The bouncers would have to kick in the cubicle doors in the jacks and pull couples out who were having a quick shag.

But Frank hadn't gone there in years.

I told Damien I'd go if he was, but I had no ID and you had to be eighteen because there was a bar.

Damien said they never looked for ID if you looked anywhere near sixteen or so.

He asked me if I wanted him to get me some cans because he was going to the off-licence. It was a good idea to get pissed before you went in, because the pints were £2.50.

I told him I wanted cans. But I didn't know how many to get.
I didn't know how many made you drunk.

I thought I'd aim high and told him to get me ten. He laughed and told me to stop messing. But I didn't know if that meant I should ask for more or less, so I asked how many he was getting.

He said four or five. I said to get me the same.

But then he said, 'What do you want?' And I said, 'Four.' And he said, 'Four what?' And I said, 'Four cans.' 'Of what?' he said.

I said Carlsberg. Advertising works.

We arranged to meet at the monument in the Christian Brothers' school where all the lunatics went.

I had to decide what to wear.

I had no good clothes.

In the end I took one of Frank's shirts.

It was black with a white pattern.

THIS LIME TREE BOWER 115

Little birds.

Actually I saw it again recently.

Stupid-looking thing.

I had a shower and put on loads of talc.

I cut myself shaving, and when I put Frank's new aftershave on, my face went all red and angry. I looked like there was something wrong with me.

Which was unfair because I was right as rain.

I got my bike out and told Dad I was calling for Fergus and Noel.

The air was frosty and there was an orange glow over the city.

But out by us you could see the stars.

I knew Damien would be late because he always was.

I locked my bike at the bottom of the monument and went up about a hundred steps to where you could sit down.

It was a great view.

In the distance I could see Dublin Bay.

All the lights. It was very peaceful.

I thought about what my wife would be like.

But she just seemed to be like me and it got a bit boring.

After about half an hour, I saw Damien coming through the gates. He had a bag with him.

He was far away and very small.

I thought that if I'd had a gun I could have shot him.

I don't know what made me think that.

He was quite drunk already.

He sat beside me and I was asking him about Shadows.

He told me that if I didn't get my end away, he'd give me a hundred quid.

He had had a bottle of wine with his mum before coming out.

I thought that was great.

Then I thought about my mum.

She would never have drunk a bottle of wine with anyone.

I was a bit nervous about drinking the Carlsberg. I had had beer a few times at home and I'd liked it.

Dad put lemonade in it.

After two cans I'd felt happier than I'd ever felt. I was in love with Damien – in a friendly way.

I wanted him to myself, if that's what love is.

I couldn't finish my last can.

We went down to our bikes and we were laughing at nothing.

We wobbled all over the road.

There was a huge queue outside Shadows.

We were waiting for about twenty minutes.

The girls had mini-skirts or leggings but only a few had nice legs.

There was too much perfume everywhere.

It was in my mouth.

The blokes looked like they'd kill you as soon as look at you.

The bouncers wouldn't let a group of fellas in. They were barred.

They started shouting and saying the bouncers were fucking dead.

I couldn't see what the big deal was.

It looked like the sort of place I'd prefer to be barred from.

When we got in we were searched.

And we had to pay six fucking quid.

The music was brutal. I was made to put my jacket in the cloakroom, and I had to pay fifty pence.

There was pink fluorescent tubing all along the walls and around the dance floor.

I was trying not to catch anyone's eye in case I got a hiding.

Damien got a drink at the bar.

He knew some girls there.

I saw him dancing.

The place got packed really quickly.

I was getting tired.

I walked around and watched everything.

There was a stool at the bar so I sat there.

But then I had to buy a drink.

I got a pint of Carlsberg.

It made me feel better.

I saw a bloke who was about twenty.

He looked like he did weights.

He was on his own dancing at the bar.

He was on something.

A girl came over to him and they started getting off. Then she got off with someone else. It was mad.

It was a shithole.

Everyone behaved like animals.

I had quite a lot of principles.

At about eleven Damien came over to me.

He was holding a girl around the waist.

She was thin and she had dyed-blonde hair.

She was smiling but she was very drunk.

Damien asked if I was ready to go.

Too fucking right I was, I told him.

He laughed.

He brought the girl out with us.

He was getting off with her while I unlocked the bikes.

She wanted us to walk her home.

She lived up near the Grange where all the knackers lived.

We walked down the dual carriageway.

They kept stopping and kissing.

We turned up by the garden centre.

There was a lane that ran up along the side of a hill.

It was really dark but it was a short cut for the Grange.

We had to go up by the old church with no roof that everyone said was haunted.

Damien told me to hang on.

The girl was nearly asleep and he took her into the graveyard.

I just wanted to go home.

I waited a few minutes because I thought they were going to the toilet.

But I got pissed off and went in to get them.

I saw something moving on a grave.

I nearly shit myself because I thought it was something crawling out of the grave.

But it was worse.

Damien had his trousers down and the girl's legs were on either side of him, like they were broken.

Her neck was on the low rail around the grave and her head hung over the gravel.

Damien was pushing into her like he wanted to put her in the ground.

I ran straight back to my bike and cycled home.

I said goodnight and got sick in the bathroom.

I wondered if the girl knew what was happening to her. I wanted to hop on my bike and go back.

But it was too late. It was pointless.

I lay in bed and I dreamed.

I saw the girl, and I saw the girl I fancied, Deborah Something, and I saw another woman in a red dress with no shoes on.

She was laughing at herself.

I woke up at four in the morning.

I stood in the kitchen drinking juice.

The horrible thing was that what I saw made me sick to my stomach, but at the same time it was really turning me on.

And that upset me.

I was in bits all that Monday in school.

Damien never came in.

I had to see him.

I wanted him to tell me the girl had a great time and he saw her home.

I didn't want to hear anything else.

I couldn't concentrate on anything.

When I got home, Dad was reading the paper.

I didn't want to speak to anybody.

I went straight to my room.

Frank and Ray were sitting on my bed.

And all over Frank's bed was the biggest load of money I'd ever seen.

RAY

It was the most bizarre fucking situation.

Head-the-Ball was after doing an armed robbery. And I'd done the getaway.

He was going mad with excitement. And I have to admit, it was fairly catching.

I was glad when Joe found us in the room because it made Frank act a bit more responsibly.

He was very straight and told Joe everything.

Joe was annoyed.

He wasn't sure whether or not Frank was taking the piss. He just didn't want to believe it. But you could see he did.

And he was shitting himself.

And this was getting on Frank's nerves and he wanted to get out of the house.

I told him he should just get back to work and pretend everything was normal.

But Frank was going mad.

So I said we could go for a quick drive.

Frank hid the money under his bed.

He had a suitcase there where he kept bits and pieces.

He'd gotten nearly thirty grand.

He made Joe come with us to make sure he didn't do anything stupid, and then we couldn't resist it, we drove by the bookies.

There were two squad cars parked outside and a guard was standing in the doorway.

A group of women had come out of their houses and they had their arms folded, talking about it.

It had only taken Frank about five minutes and he was sure no one had seen him.

No one was going to believe he'd done it anyway.

He kept telling it over and over and turning the radio on and off.

Joe was quiet at first, but then he started asking questions.

We drove along the coast.

Frank and Joe started to laugh at the whole thing.

Lunatics. But we all had different natures.

For now I was happy to roll along merrily and not get to upset.

I don't get upset much.

But the more Joe was asking what we should do next, the more I was beginning to see what a good fucking question it was.

I have that sort of philosophical training.

So after driving around for a while I decided that enough was enough.

It was getting a bit stupid.

I pulled over and told them what to do.

Absolutely nothing.

They had to go back and pretend nothing had happened. Listen to what people said, what the local theories were, and cultivate them.

They had to see which way the cookie bounced.

The last thing they wanted to do was a *Thelma and Louise* job.

Only a stupid prick would take off.

In a way, I wanted them off my back.

I didn't need the hassle.

So we went back to the chipper, and of course, I was right.

There wasn't a stir in the place.

Why would there be?

No guards had come. No nothing.

I had a bite with Joe and Frank got back to work.

People were coming in for their tea and asking Frank if he'd heard about the bookies.

And Frank was all, 'Yeah, what happened exactly?'

And the stories were all different.

Someone said it was a gang of raiders who'd gotten away in a car.

Someone else said the robbers had a stick of dynamite and they'd threatened to blow up the safe if McCurdie didn't open it.

Some fucking eejit with a woolly hat said a shot had been fired into the ceiling and the guards were looking for fingerprints on the bullet.

Joe was laughing but Frank kept a straight face. And I knew he'd be okay.

And later on when Carmel came home, we went up to her room.

What a beautiful girl she was.

What a fit girl.

Well.

In the morning there was a message on my machine from Tony Reagan.

He wanted to apologise for what had happened at the staff meeting.

He hoped I understood that it was Konigsberg who'd insisted on giving his papers with no discussion.

There was very little Tony could do but he would try to have a word.

I rang him back. I was gracious and I told him not to worry.

When I got into my office there was a note slipped under the door.

It was from the third-year I'd slept with. She had wanted to meet me the night before. Well, too late now.

I fucked it in the bin.

I didn't have her in any classes that week and I'm going to be completely frank with you here. I didn't really like her.

And I have the guts to admit that, you know?

I took out the two books of collected papers I had by Konigsberg.

He had been developing this brutal theory since the fifties.

He said that language was an organic thing, like any plant or animal. And just like any plant or animal, it was born, lived healthily for a while, making other little languages, like its offspring, and then it died. Same as everything else.

And our language is dying now.

No one talks properly.

There is a lack of sincerity, he claimed, because language is sick now.

It isn't vital enough to sustain validity.

Politicians are elected on saying the right thing strategically, not morally.

People in general aren't reading.

The action movie has replaced poetry.

People can't make an effort to be entertained.

They take drugs instead.

Blah, blah, blah, language is dying.

Now this meant that Konigsberg was either very clever or very lucky.

Because it made him hard to categorise.

He was a sort of Aristotelian, Darwinian, Marxist, Communitarian type thing.

And I don't know how much money he'd made hawking this notion around the lecture circuit. But I'd say it would have to be something pretty fucking amazing.

Tony Reagan knocked in to see me.

He'd just been on to Konigsberg's personal secretary or agent, or whatever she was.

And lo and behold, he had agreed to a very brief question-and-answer session after his last lecture.

I told Tony I owed him one.

But he said he was looking forward to it.

It'd be entertaining to say the least.

But I knew if I could nail Konigsberg, they'd be writing articles about me for years.

When he finally arrived, there was a big buzz in the college.

You see, nearly every department found him relevant, literature, linguistics, history, philosophy, everybody.

They had his first lecture in the evening so all the students would get a chance to see him.

He was in the largest lecture theatre but it was so full they had to rig up a closed-circuit system to the next theatre, where everyone could see him on a huge screen.

With the question-and-answer session not happening till the third lecture I wasn't bothered going to the first two.

Anyway the thought of watching all those morons slobbering all over Konigsberg annoyed me.

And it made me jealous. I admit it.

It did.

There was a sort of reception thing after each lecture, which I did go to.

There was free wine and sandwiches.

Konigsberg was never there.

He needed his rest. Only post-graduates were supposed to be at these receptions and there were academics from all over Europe there especially.

But a bunch of philosophy students who were in with the department always blagged their way in to get locked.

So you had to be quick.

I got completely rat-arsed and all around me twits tried to be clever and funny.

I made a point of getting into a row and left. On the way home I phoned Frank to get the lowdown.

Everything was cool.

People saw the robbery as one of those things that happen, and that's life and it was a learning experience and that was that.

But at the same time, Frank was nervous and excited and he wanted to do something.

He wanted to unwind. He wanted to get away.

I didn't want him doing anything thick so I told him we could drive down the country at the weekend. Me, him and Joe.

That way I could keep an eye on them.

Konigsberg's last lecture was on Friday morning and I arranged to pick them up after that.

That was the plan.

On Thursday night, I was at another wine and shite-talk reception.

A bottle and a half into the proceedings and I spot the third-year chick.

And she was pretending not to see me.

I ask you.

And may God forgive me, but with every glass of Ernest and Julio Gallo, her tits were getting more imperative.

So I fucked over to the student bar with her and her bunch of know-it-all shitbrain friends.

And there we are, pint after pint and she's sitting beside me with her great big legs in knee-high boots.

And I'm getting a dirty mind and I know that if I don't get it in her in the next few minutes, I'm going to give someone a dig.

So we split and I'm giving her a lift home.

And her hand is down my pants and I open them up and Jesus Christ, she's sucking me like a starving baby.

So we get to her place, I'm fucked.

She carries me up the stairs into her room.

And I remember I was really interested in her keeping her boots on.

And I was just pulling off her knickers and the door burst open.

And this little fellow with long hair ran in, going berserk.

He jumped on me and she was shouting, 'Vyvyan, No!' He pushes me out into the landing.

I was trying to pull my pants up, and I fell down the stairs on to the hall table.

The phone flew off and went through the glass in the front door.

And I needn't tell you, I was out into the car like a bullet.

I locked my door and your man was banging on the roof. I reversed at about fifty miles an hour. I didn't even look.

I skidded across the street and got it into first. Vyvyan jumps in front of the car.

I put the foot down.

I'm not sure, but I think I might have clipped him. I wasn't going back to check.

I had a big day in the morning.

I was getting an early night.

When I got home I threw some stuff into a bag for going away with the boys.

Then I lay in the bath and I was dreaming about Martha Nussbaum.

We were talking about Aristotle and getting ready to go to bed for a shag and she lifted up her dress and she had a dick.

I jumped and woke up.

It was nearly two o'clock in the morning and the bath was freezing.

I poured myself a large glass of medicinal brandy, went to bed and shivered myself to sleep.

The alarm went off.

Ten o'clock.

Konigsberg's lecture was at eleven.

And Jesus Christ, early night or not, after all the wine and beer and brandy, not to mention lying in a cold bath for half the night, I was completely bollocksed.

I had an hour, but I could hardly fucking move.

I had a shower and a shave.

Tried to have a shit but nothing was happening.

I was in bits.

On the way into college I stopped for petrol and got some Solpadeine and juice.

I put the carton to my mouth and I swear to God I couldn't stop drinking until the entire litre was gone. I was that dehydrated.

The lecture theatre was full of nobodies all out for as much enlightenment as their little heads could handle.

And there he was.

Professor Wolfgang Konigsberg was about five foot and completely bald.

He sounded like Spike Milligan doing Hitler impressions. I could hardly hear what he was saying.

It was giving me a headache.

Everyone was watching him intently.

Some were even nodding in agreement, going, 'Mmm, mmm.'

It would make you sick.

The third-year chick was looking over at me. She was sobbing into a little piece of toilet roll.

I was beginning to feel worse.

There a gurgling sound coming from my stomach. There were waves of nausea.

I was sweating but my feet were freezing.

I closed my eyes.

Then there was applause and I heard Tony Reagan say, 'Professor Konigsberg has very kindly agreed to take one or two questions. And I know that Dr Raymond Sullivan would like to ask the first one.'

That was me.

My eyes were watering.

My head felt lighter than my body.

And I was sitting in the middle of a row.

I couldn't get out.

Everyone looked at me expectantly.

Konigsberg was looking around, wondering who was going to say something.

And then, absolutely beyond my control, a long stream of orange puke shot out of my mouth.

It sailed across the room and all over the people for about ten feet in front of me.

I spluttered for a moment, and coughed a little, and then there was complete silence.

I immediately felt much better.

I wiped my face and looked around.

No one could believe what they had just seen.

I stood up and cleared my throat.

'Yes. Thank you, Professor Reagan,' I said. 'I would like to ask Professor Konigsberg if, during his long and eminent career, he has ever seen anything expressed quite like that.'

Tony Reagan didn't know what to do.

He just looked at Konigsberg.

The smell of sick was rising through the room.

Konigsberg didn't say anything.

And then, finally, he slowly shook his head.

I thanked him politely and made my way out.

I couldn't even remember what I had wanted to say.

Fuck it.

FRANK (*to Ray*)

I never heard that.

RAY

I've been saving it.

FRANK

It was a weird feeling.

I had thirty thousand pounds under my bed.

The first thing I did, the evening of the robbery, was bury the gun.

I took it up to the hill before the Grange and dug a hole under a tree in the woods.

I wasn't sure what to do with the money though. I didn't want to bury it in case it was too hard to get when I needed it.

And I was afraid to lodge it in case some case I knew at the bank got suspicious.

I was even afraid to look at it.

So it just lay there under the bed.

But no one was on to me and that was obvious.

About the Wednesday, Simple Simon and Charlie came in for their lunch.

They were very quiet.

They'd lost their swagger.

I was a smart-arse.

I was all, 'Do you think they'll catch whoever did it, Mr McCurdie?'

And he was, 'I don't honestly think so, Frank, I really don't.'

Charlie couldn't understand how the robber had disappeared after running down the lane.

'I nearly had the bastard, Frank,' he said. 'I was about as close to him as I am to you now.' Which was too fucking true.

Simon was telling Charlie not to blame himself. There was nothing he could have done. And I was agreeing with them.

But I was sick to the gills when I thought about how lucky I'd been.

If Ray hadn't come I was fucked.

And what good had it done?

How could I pay Dad's loan off?

Everyone would know it was me.

I was getting restless.

Joe was moping around in the dumps all the time and I couldn't cheer him up.

I was hoping it wasn't my fault.

But sometimes you have to decide that principles will only fuck you up, because no one else is ever moral.

I wanted to give Joe some cash.

I didn't know what I wanted.

When we were in bed one night, I said I hoped he wasn't angry at me.

But he wasn't.

He told me about seeing some eejit from his school having it off with a knacker from the Grange. It had really upset him.

But I couldn't see the big deal and I didn't know what to say to him.

I was annoyed at him.

But then that night I was thinking about a woman I knew when I was Joe's age.

I used to wash her windows and cut the grass.

She had two young children and her husband was a plumber.

I sometimes used to walk with her to collect her kids from school.

And then one day, in her kitchen, she touched my hand and I never went back.

I was going to tell Joe this, but he was asleep. I didn't see what it had to do with him anyway.

I decided we should get away for a few days.

I asked Ray. His car would give us that aimless millionaire feeling I was after.

I told Carmel I wanted her to work with Dad for the weekend.

She went bananas because she had an exam coming up. But I told her that Joe needed a break from his studying and she could be a Christian for five minutes.

That got her. She was guilty about Joe not having a mother, and she was always fighting with him.

I know it was mean, but she felt it and you've got to use what you've got.

I waited until Dad was into the second half of the bottle before I said anything.

He smiled. He thought it was a good idea.

What a great man. He made me proud.

I couldn't leave the money under the bed for the weekend. So me and Joe put it all into plastic bags with some stones, then we sealed them with elastic bands and put them in the tank up in the attic.

And when we came back down, it hit us that we should have taken some out for the weekend. We got all giggly and we were wondering how much we should take.

We didn't know, so we guessed on five grand.

Joe was cheering up.

I told him not to go into school on Friday because Ray would be picking us up at lunchtime.

In the morning I was washing the floor and the old man came over and handed me fifty quid. Of course, I was saying, 'No, no.' But he wouldn't take it back. 'For a drink,' he kept saying, 'Buy a round.' Then he winked at me and walked off.

It was the first time I'd felt guilty.

That man had done everything by the rules in his life and look what happened.

He was left on his own and shagged by bastards like McCurdie.

But he was right. That was the thing.

Well I didn't want to be right any more.

That's a load of meaningless toss.

I was glad when Ray showed up.

He looked like shit.

He was having a whiskey with Dad while I went to get changed.

Joe came in and told me Dad had given him twenty quid. He felt really guilty as well.

We broke our shit laughing.

We put the gear in the car and we were trying to decide where to go.

We hadn't thought about it.

Joe just said, 'Cork,' and that was it.

We were off.

It felt good to be moving.

We were taking the piss out of Marian Finucane on the radio.

They were going on about planning permission for sheds and extensions.

Ray said he'd give her shed an extension if she didn't shut the fuck up.

He had it in for everybody.

He was in bad humour because he was hungover.

So we stopped in Abbeyleix for a cure.

I wasn't sure how to treat Joe in this respect. But he just asked us what we wanted and bought the first round.

I was relieved.

The last thing I wanted was to have to be his parent. He had to grow up. Let him.

It was very nice there and we didn't want to go. But Cork it was and off we went.

I asked Ray which was the most expensive hotel. We could afford it.

Me and Joe shared a room.

Old habits.

And Ray got himself a double room, because, as he put it, you never know.

Joe was having a bath and I took Ray aside to give him a grand for the weekend.

He didn't want it, but I made him take it. We were like children playing.

We had a drink sent up to the room and Ray toasted me.

He said I was the weirdest bastard he'd ever met.

At nine we went down and had a beautiful dinner. We got champagne, but only Ray liked it. Me and Joe thought it was horrible.

Ray said we were the typical nouveau riche, all money and no taste.

Fuck him. We had pints.

Afterwards we headed into town.

Most of the pubs were packed but we found a little auldfellas' place that served us till about half twelve.

Back at the hotel there was a disco.

We got a drink and Ray started talking to a girl around Joe's age, and I don't know what he said to her, maybe he paid her, I don't know. But she came over, asked Joe to dance and got off with him the whole evening.

Joe was beaming when we went to bed.

But then he said he missed her.

Everything backfires.

You can't do fucking anything.

And that was what the weekend was like.

We were the boys.

Rested and refreshed.

Until we got back on Sunday evening and there was a squad car outside the chipper.

JOE

When we saw the guards, I think we all had the same idea.

To put the foot down and get out of there.

But it was too late. They saw us.

It was horrible.

Ray pulled over and a sergeant asked us to come in.

There was a detective sitting with Dad in the front room. Dad looked wrecked.

Carmel glared at us.

Frank was white and his hands were shaking.

But we were all completely wrong.

Because it was me the detective wanted to talk to. He asked me if I knew a girl called Sarah Comisky.

I didn't, I'd never heard the name.

Then he asked me if I ever went to Shadows nightclub.

I looked at Dad, but I had to say yes.

He asked was I there the previous Sunday.

I said I was and he nodded.

He just wanted to talk to me and Dad.

Everyone else had to go.

And when they were gone, he said I'd been accused of raping Sarah Comisky.

I nearly fell on the floor.

I said it wasn't me.

I didn't know any Sarahs.

But the detective told me to relax.

The girl hadn't accused me.

Damien had.

She had been attacked up in the graveyard near the Grange.

She had identified Damien as her attacker, but he said it was me.

The girl was very drunk but she did remember someone else being there.

So the guards wanted to find out if both of us had done it, or if one, which one.

Dad came with me down to the station and I had to give my account of what had happened. They made sure I got all the details right and then they gave me a cup of tea and a Kit Kat.

Then Dad signed something, then I did and they took a blood test.

Then we could go home.

I couldn't believe Damien had dropped me in it like that.

But Dad said I was too naive and that people would do anything to save their skin.

He said he knew it was disappointing but that was the way it was.

At home we all sat up late and talked about it and everyone was great.

We all drank beer until very late in the morning.

In bed that night I thought about my mother. It wasn't about the times when she couldn't talk and gave me nightmares.

It was about another time I'd forgotten.

Dad was teaching me how to skim stones on the beach. And Mum was trying to do it and she couldn't.

It was summer and she had a red dress on.

Dad was slagging her and she was laughing at herself.

And I felt safe and the safe feeling stayed.

I didn't go to school that week and the guards called on Tuesday to say that my test was negative.

They were charging Damien.

There was a bit of a shindig in the house.

Frank told me he was putting money away for me to go to college, but I wasn't to say anything to Dad.

And Frank went to Chicago a few weeks later and he sent money back for Dad to pay off his loan.

Maybe he had a job, maybe he didn't.

Dad wasn't to know.

Ray brought a book out which nobody read.

But he was pleased.

He said that that was the point.

So in the end it was like things started off good, and just got better.

Is that cheating?

I don't know.

It's hard to say.

I can still see the girl.

ST NICHOLAS

For Paddy Breathnach and Robert Walpole

St Nicholas was first performed at the Bush Theatre, London, on 19 February 1997.

Performer   Brian Cox
Director   Conor McPherson
Lighting Designer   Paul Russell

The play was written while Conor McPherson was attached to the Bush Theatre under the Pearson Television Theatre Writers' Scheme.

A MAN, *late fifties*

A bare stage

Part One

When I was a boy, I was afraid of the dark . . . What was there.

And maybe one of the things I thought was there was vampires.

I don't know. I can't remember now.

But like all of us, whatever idea I did have about them, it was probably all the superstitious bullshit we get in books. And fiction. But that was nothing like the real thing. Like anything, the real thing is a lot more ordinary.

It's a 'matter of fact'. Matter of fact.

And that's far more frightening than anything you can make up.

Because it's real.

It's just there. Casual as everything else. Just waiting to be dealt with.

And there are practical things to be learned. Yes indeed.

Back in those days I was a fat bastard.

And I had a big red mush from drinking.

This is back before I met the vampires.

Before I knew what power was and what evil was.

But back then I thought I knew everything.

And I had lots of what I thought power was.

Because I was a theatre critic.

I was a journalist. I was a lucky bastard. I was blessed, or cursed, whichever, with the ability to string words together. I could string words together.

And that's all it was.

I mean, I was intelligent, but I had no real thoughts about things.

I'd never taken the care to form an opinion. I just had them.

And only one care in the world, when I think back on it now, me.

I wanted . . . everything.

Love, I suppose. Respect. Esteem.

But I didn't deserve it. No, I don't think I deserved any respect. But I got it.

Oh yeah. I got it. Because people were afraid of me. I loved it. Going to big productions. Big names.

Careers spanning tens of glittering years.

And everyone afraid of what I'd write?

Of what I 'liked'?

And I hardly really liked anything.

And even when I did like something, mostly what I felt was . . . jealous.

I had tried writing.

Tried to convey the feelings I had.

That I genuinely fucking had – for people.

I loved people. I loved the stupid bastards.

But. I had no ideas.

No ideas for a story.

I wanted to let my compassion seep out across the stage.

Handicapped people in love.

Queers and lesbians absolving each other.

A liberal, fucking, all-encompassing . . . you know.

But nothing came.

Nothing ever came.

I could only write about what there was already. I was a hack. And I was drunk. I was at gallery openings, milling free glasses of wine. I was in the bar after the premiere of plays.

I was the educated friend of the masses who read me. Protecting them from these artistic charlatans who were trying to rob their money.

And I could feel this . . . light. Going out. I could feel it.

It was panic I suppose.

Getting older, nothing done yet.

I started rows with directors in pubs.

I walked out of plays ten minutes before the end. I was on the telly.

I had all this drive, going nowhere. It was putting me in the ground.

And I'd get a fright you see. And I'd drink. And when I drank I always got vicious hangovers. And I'd be useless. Couldn't do a thing. Just do it again.

And you see, my life was quite conducive to that. There wasn't a problem.

I only needed to get about one solid hour done in a day. And then I was free.

I rehashed columns.

I usually had reviews written before the show was finished.

I could leaf through a current affairs magazine, see something, half an hour, I'd have a thousand words.

Tide me over.

And I was probably in the top-five highest-paid in the paper. You know? Editors licked the hole off me.

I was a character.

Famous in all the wrong ways. Nobody went without.

Not my fat tracksuit wife.

She didn't want anything.

She was happy enough to get a half-bottle of gin into her.

And the days just slipped through her thick fingers.

Big house in the right place.

The cars and the cash. We were a pair of fat fuckers rolling around in the mud.

And our kids.

My girl was at college.

I loved her. I loved her in that way I couldn't look her in the eye, you know? I couldn't find the words.

It was too late. I just left money on the kitchen table every week.

Apparently she was a brilliant student and I suspected she was a writer but I don't think I could have faced it if she was. You know? I avoided her.

I sat in my study with Milton and Chaucer, nice and cosy. And I'd finish a bottle and hit the sack at two or three.

And then I'd hear my boy come in.

He did nothing and I supported it.

All I knew was he stank of deodorant and he had some fruitless ambition to be a musician. Plinking away at that hour of the night.

He didn't want anything to do with me. And even now my face is burning when I think about my children.

And my stomach is like a brick wall.

Well I'd be too drunk to hear my wife snoring for long and I'd lie in the dark with morning coming.

She knew better than to try and touch me. And I would remember that I loved her once, when we were young. We used to sit in her house and everything outside was made for us. All we had to do was keep holding hands. And I couldn't even do that.

No, what I could do was sit in those yellow bars. With the journalists. Men falling in their pints. There was a breed of us, you see, and we weren't mere reporters.

We had columns.

There'd be a gang.

Men and women.

The women just on the verge of going to seed. Just on the brink, you understand.

And I was a big shot in those places. I could've had my pick.

I knew I could.

Those women with buckles on their shoes and their bows all done wrong.

They had each other, those journalists. There were one or two young things in the bloom of youth, but then the responsibility, you see, the responsibility got them. They were expected to have an opinion. On everything.

They were expected to be on top of situations and the current . . . goings-on.

Otherwise, what justified their existence?

The man in the street needed to know what to think, hence these objective observers. And that may have partly been their fucking . . . thing.

But the other was the pressure to fill space. Just fill column inches. It's not a pleasant feeling.

You've got to fill it with words.

And these kids could never admit they couldn't find the news. They all used to rob each other.

They'd be dizzy for a year or two. All aflutter with responsibility.

And then all asunder with it.

And then the weight would pile on. Because there was a need for stimulation, wasn't there?

It became more and more that it was easier to stay in town than go home.

A few scoops at teatime.

And then, time to eat. Money to lose.

And, you fell in with another journalist, as a lover, you were a goner.

Because you'd help each other to keep going. And you'd look at each other with a joyous tear of camaraderie. And then a bawling hatred because . . . well, because you knew this was hell.

Of course it wasn't all like that.

Newspapers wouldn't get printed if it was. There wasn't many of us.

But enough. Enough drunken pig-headedness being passed off as authority.

That's the way I perceived it.

That was the world I was in.

Fuck. You think I was going to surround myself with people who were succeeding?

And what was I like in those places . . .

I wasn't dying, like you might think.

No. I was dead.

And every so often, I get it. I'd smell the rot. And the Scotch'd start disappearing fairly fucking sharpish.

Mmm. I was a bollocks to all the other critics.

And I'll tell you why, because it was this: they were all cunts.

Well. I couldn't stand their wishy-washiness. They were always looking for an angle. Like children jumping up behind each other to see a parade.

Like the kids filling space.

But most of all I hated them because I wanted them to like me.

But all I was good at was being noticed. The only way I knew how.

By being . . . well, I'd never sit beside another critic.

All that effort being put into being . . . a type of thing.

I had none left for at home.

I would wake up and 'do some work'.

Do an hour.

And my wife would make some lunch for me. And she would sit with me.

She wanted me to say something.

And I could taste her care.

And I'd munch it down.

What are you going to do?

You've got to keep it in, haven't you?

You open those floodgates, Christ knows what the hell is going to come pouring out.

So, it was into town. Stick the head in the office. A few likely recruits.

And a quick jaunt down to wherever the fuck you reckoned you weren't going to be poisoned by the beer.

And I think we took comfort from being in those places.

Where at one time, genius was at work. Or play or . . . Kavanagh, O'Nolan, and what have you.

You know, that it was still possible to produce enduring works even though you were hungover or drunk, even. And then you began to think that it was the only way to produce enduring works.

But, there was nothing noble about those writers waking up at dawn, pissed out of their bins, groping around for the bottle they'd taken home, putting their hand in the puke that had finally let them sleep.

But we'd keep it up . . . all this.

Until nobody really fucking cared any more.

And then I'd shoot off down to the Project or the Peacock to witness another amateur disaster.

And on, and on, and on.

But this was before I met the vampires, before I worked for them.

Before I had to fight for anything.

It was a girl that got me into trouble.

Unintentionally. It was my fault.

She was an up-and-coming actress.

I was reviewing a new production of *Salome* at the Abbey.

And when she danced. Fuck me.

I mean, shadows crept about the muscles of her legs. Her arms. Even her fingers had such . . . She was just one more fucking . . . thing beyond my reach.

But I had underestimated my reviewing . . . capacity.

One of my very few moments of modesty.

Back in those days.

It was after the show in The Flowing Tide.

I'd made it for last orders.

My review was already phoned in.

I'd written it on the back of my programme during the show.

Then I rang it in from my car.

And that was the end of that. That was the way I did it.

It was the best of everything.

I could stand there with the cast and ruin their evening. And get paid for it.

I was feeling generous that night.

I gave them a mixed review.

It was twenty past when I got to the pub.

I got two pints and two double Jemmies.

Now I could relax.

I knew Peter Hamilton, the director, from a few years before when I'd been speaking at a symposium on Irish theatre.

He was a prick.

He came over to me.

The cast were mostly in one corner.

I saw the actress who'd played Salome.

Her name was Helen.

I saw her glance over.

Hamilton said he was surprised to see me there. 'Why?' I said.

I had no time for him.

But plenty of time to make that clear, if you know what I mean.

'Were you not reviewing us tonight?' he said. Awful high-pitched voice.

I told him the review was gone in and if he nipped over to the paper he could probably get tomorrow's edition.

'Ah, no rush,' he said.

But I could see him getting a little bit restless.

He had no cop.

I knew he was going to give in and ask me. And he did.

'If it's already gone in,' he said, 'you might as well tell me what you thought.'

And then he gave a little laugh like none of this mattered, and he took a big gulp from his pint.

'What I thought.' I said.

I was pretending I'd given it so much consideration it was hard to sum up now.

'Yes,' I said, 'Well I think it's one of the best shows I've seen in years and anybody who knows what's what would be a fool to miss it.'

Well. Hamilton could hardly contain himself. He made the effort to stick around and make a bit of chit-chat with me, but as soon as he got the chance he shot off to tell the others.

And that's how the party got going.

A kind of euphoria spread quite quickly and even the barmen didn't seem to want to stop serving.

I got chatting to the cast.

Drinks were placed in front of me.

I even began to believe my own hype. I began to think I had given it a good review.

I was walking around congratulating everybody. 'My life has been changed,' I told them.

They hugged me and I wept.

Why I wept I don't know.

Just an accumulation of drink and aggravated lying, I suppose, but I did.

And it worked and they all thought I was great.

I was different from the other critics who didn't know what they were talking about.

I had a passionate belief in the theatre and what makes it good.

And then we were out in the street and I was tired.

They wanted to go on somewhere else but I knew I was finished.

And anyway it was only a matter of time before someone got their hands on the paper and saw what a lying bastard I was.

I leaned against the car and bid them goodnight.

And off they went.

And then, a cool hand.

Helen.

'I think I'll go home as well,' she said.

I asked her where she lived.

Donnybrook. It was on my way.

Next thing, she was sitting beside me and we were driving through the empty streets.

You know that way?

And I couldn't help taking a sneaky look at her legs.

And I drove fairly slowly.

We didn't talk.

I badly, badly wanted to tell her the truth.

But I wasn't able to.

This was my moment and . . . I may never be that close to her again.

You know?

When we'd stop at the lights and this, I'd be giving her friendly . . . you know? Smiling at her.

Chaucer and Milton were in the back of the car. Having a great fucking time.

But this was just a lift home.

Let's not get excited.

Dropped her off in Pembroke Park.

She kissed me on the cheek before she got out. And I was the lowest thing.

'Good luck tomorrow night,' I said.

And she told me to sleep well.

I couldn't sleep.

I sat in my study with the windows open. That summer breeze.

And I thought about killing myself. I could imagine the cast reading the review I'd actually given them, talking about what a complete cunt I was. And then they'd find out I was dead and they'd feel rotten. That they hadn't taken into account the integrity you know? The mystery that I was. But I was too chicken for that.

Instead I lay on the sofa and things crawled all over me till it got bright.

Well. I wasn't the same after that.

The summer, all our prospects, that bright youthful . . .

I was hacking away, reviewing books. On the radio, what have you.

And I couldn't stop thinking about her. I'd be working and suddenly I'd remember her and be all . . . fucking hell.

Happy. But that tinge as well.

Wasn't a sexual thing.

If she were ever to give herself to me, it'd be her acceptance of me. My fat, blotchy skin wasn't the point.

I don't think I even wanted that.

I knew that when we were married, I'd be happy enough just to sit and watch her tend our beautiful children.

Yeah.

Well the show didn't get any good reviews as it turned out, but the news was it was doing two weeks in London, knocked down from an intended four.

I went back to the Abbey the night it closed.

Broke my fucking heart to watch her.

And I'll tell you, because it was in her arms.

Because you could see her arms working. The weight changing there.

With you and me, it's all this:

We get older, we try to hide the excess. We compensate for our appearance with our 'sense of humour' or our taste, or our . . . mind.

But what if you woke up in the morning and you were the physical specimen you always wanted to be.

Wouldn't that make you happy? Of course it would.

Go a long way in any case.

Because now your smile would beam confidence. Your stride would never need to conceal the way you were built.

And we could all concentrate on just being nice to each other.

This is all getting very Nazi now. But Helen had that.

She was never conscious of herself, because everybody else was busy doing that for her. Do you see?

You probably don't.

But that's why when she smiled at you, you knew you were blessed because her will was pure. She had nothing to hide.

Here was this person doing what they wanted, no more and no less.

And to be that thing that she wanted? Well, then you'd stop performing like a fucking monkey.

And that's a peace few of us ever find.

Hmm?

And you could see all that in the assured grace of her arms.

And the way they moved.

And to be in those arms . . .

The next morning I packed a few things. I was going to London.

I left the house like I would any day. My boy was still in bed.

I'd heard him bring a girl in around four and I hadn't heard her leave.

My daughter was gone hours ago.

I wanted to see her before I went.

I was afraid I wasn't going to see her again.

I remembered when she was a little thing.

Crawling into bed beside me on a stormy night.

My hand up the back of her T-shirt. My hand wider than her back.

Her little feet on my knee.

My wife was out the back doing her flowers.

I watched her for a minute.

She was kneeling with a trowel.

She stopped and pushed her glasses up her nose with the back of her wrist. I didn't feel anything. I just left.

And nothing could have prepared me for the mad . . . fucking . . . things that were going to happen.

That's always the way. It's probably better.

I went to the bank, and then I went to the airport.

I was supposed to be reviewing some lunchtime shite in Bewley's.

And knowing I'd be up in the air by the time it went on, gave me a great, reckless . . .

I was doing something.

There wasn't a cloud in the sky. I was cradled up there.

I think I wanted it to crash.

But then the ground was solid, and this was real.

The air in London was heavy and still. I checked into a hotel and I went for a drink.

I wanted to find out where the cast were staying. Get Helen on her own. Be honest about it. Had to get busy doing this. Had to get busy, and I'll tell you why because I didn't have a clue what the hell I was going to say to her.

I had a day before they arrived for rehearsals.

I did a little bit of relaxing.

Browsed in bookshops.

Sat in pubs. Walked around.

Down the Kings Road, across the Thames, into Battersea. Not the best.

Took the bus back.

I saw the sights.

And I dumped my suit.

It was one I'd had for fifteen years.

Another quirk you see. I was full of that.

Had to get some natty duds. Impress the ladies. Changing in a little cubicle.

Caught myself in the mirror.

Belly like a mountain. Little tits and everything. Suit hid it. But the heat.

Got a linen jacket. And I went drinking.

And back at the hotel, in the early hours,

I took some hotel paper, hotel pen.

Coleridge on my shoulder.

Wrote a poem.

By the time I lay down, there was no paper left. It was all in the bin.

And the big day dawned.

I had a dirty big fry and two pots of tea. Didn't feel like the food of love.

I went down to the theatre, had a walk around.

I saw the scenery go in. And crates.

There was a pub across the road.

I had a quick couple of pints. Back out, walking around. No sign of the cast. Couple more pints.

Thinking about my editor and my wife. Wondering where I was. I'd had binges before. Not to worry, you know? It was that way. Be ringing each other. I never understood why she stayed.

What she saw in me. I couldn't see it.

The cast began to arrive in twos and threes up out of the Tube.

But no Helen. She was another hour and a half. Arrived in a taxi. With Peter Hamilton.

What the fuck was this, you know?

She waited for him while he paid the fare. Then she linked his arm and they went inside. I went back in the pub and had a quick double, a bracer.

What were they doing together, you know? Maybe it was nothing.

A little fling at best.

Hamilton abusing his position. He was probably gay anyway.

And theatre people fuck like rabbits. Bucking each other up.

Didn't mean a thing. Nothing.

Compared to what I felt.

Another quick bracer.

At teatime they began to emerge. They were in good form. They were coming into the pub. I lashed out and bought a tweed hat.

I pulled it down low and sat in a corner watching them over a newspaper.

Helen was surrounded by men.

It was so obvious. They kept touching her. It was hard to look at.

Finally Hamilton ordered them all to go home about ten.

They had a heavy day tomorrow.

This was it.

Helen left with Hamilton and two other actresses. I followed them.

We all took a Tube to Victoria.

They were quiet. They were tired.

We changed trains. Main line.

Out into the suburbs. Out into Kent.

They got out near Bromley.

Went to a little terraced house.

I nipped into a shop, got a cheap bottle of Scotch. Needed a bracer for this. I sat on the road and swigged for a little while. Maybe an hour.

And then, when I couldn't feel my heart any more, I went to the house.

They must have been in bed.

Took a while to get an answer.

One of the other actresses, Cliona Leeson, opened the door.

She had a jacket on over her pyjamas. She didn't recognise me with my hat. Peter Hamilton came down behind her, protecting the women.

I took off the hat and offered them the bottle. 'Greetings,' I said

'Oh my God,' said Hamilton, 'What are you doing here?'

'Just a social call,' I said, 'And I'm looking for the chance to apologise for what my editor did to your review. He was at the show and he didn't agree with me at all.'

Hamilton wasn't sure if this was a dream.

'He changed your review?' he said.

'I'm afraid so,' I said, 'He's always fancied himself. So, naturally, I've resigned from the paper, and here I am. Can I come in?' Hamilton didn't have a choice.

He wasn't the assertive type.

'Just for a minute,' I said, 'I realise it's very late.'

Cliona Leeson yawned and went back upstairs. Left poor Hamilton to deal with this on his own.

He led me into a tiny sitting room, separated from the kitchen by a counter with stools, for playing at being out.

I made myself comfortable and Hamilton just stood smiling at me. Appalled.

He asked me if I'd like a cup of tea, but I was fine.

He gave me a glass for the Scotch.

And I offered him a drink. He needed it. 'I'll tell you, Peter,' I said, 'I've decided to come over to spread the word about the fantastic production you've done. The dogs in the street should beat down the doors to see it.'

I was making as much noise as I could, you understand. I was waking the house. Helen would know I'd come for her. And I bellowed.

'What nobody seems to realise, Peter, is that you are probably the foremost director of your generation. But they're fools, aren't they? They're blind! They must be! You're the voice in the wilderness, aren't you?' I heard movement upstairs. Cliona Leeson was telling the others.

They were getting curious.

And I continued my tirade and tore into the bottle. I was even beginning to enjoy myself. But although Hamilton was stupid, he wasn't a complete idiot, and only a complete idiot could fail to see that his work was mediocre at best.

At fucking best, mediocre.

So much as he wanted to believe what I was saying, I was, in fact, making him very miserable.

But I couldn't give a fuck.

I was here to see Helen.

And sure enough, after a while, the girls had worked up their nerve.

There were footsteps on the stairs.

So they had a big day tomorrow. They had to work. But they were on tour, they were open to new experiences.

There may well be a story in all of this.

A famous theatre story.

The critic came to apologise.

Of course they'd come down. And down they came. Three shivering actresses.

Helen looked tired. She didn't look too good. And, when she looked at me, there was nothing,

And my resolve began to crumble, only slightly, but when I told them the 'review being changed' story, I told it falteringly.

And I was running out of things to say about it. I had resigned on their behalf.

On behalf of a production that wouldn't even exist in two weeks.

It sounded like the lie it was.

But I was in for a penny now.

Hamilton wanted to believe me. I think.

It would do his career a world of good.

A critic resigning for his sake. He'd hang on to it.

Cliona Leeson seemed to be amused.

She was smirking into her cup.

Poor Helen looked too exhausted to care. But the third actress, Sheila Kilmeady, she was older. I knew her husband. He did a lot of television. I'd poured a pint over him about ten years before, at a time when I did that sort of thing because it got me the attention I wanted. And I'd brutalised him in the paper for a cameo he did in a British sitcom.

I'd said he was about as funny as wiping your hole with a Brillo Pad.

God knows why I picked on him.

But we all need a purpose in life, even if we've got to make it up, ah?

And now, here was his wife, looking at me with all that sage wisdom culchies get when they move to the city and find out that saying smart-arse crap for tourists isn't enough any more. You have to work. And life is hard. And all that shit.

'You seem to have a problem with me taking a stand, Sheila,' I said.

She looked at me for a moment and then she said, 'I just don't believe you, that's all.' And she went to bed.

Nobody said anything. It was all fucked now. Cliona Leeson and Helen followed her. Hamilton told me I was welcome to the couch. I thanked him and then I was on my own. And I realised how pissed I was. I knew I didn't want to be there in the morning. But. Helen. I'd . . . I'd . . . come to . . .

I'd come to say it.

Even if she was like them.

Even if she hated me. I'd come to say it. All I had to do was wait till they were asleep, talk to her on her own.

And maybe, why not? She'd pull back the covers and let me in and . . . Well. I don't know what. First things first. I had to wait.

So I sat there. And I drank. And I dropped off. I didn't dream. It was just black.

I felt something wet and I woke up.

I'd spilled the rest of the whisky down my pants.

It was a quarter to six.

I stood up and I nearly fell over.

I went to the sink and I puked raw whisky.

Burned the fucking throat off me.

I needed the toilet, I wasn't well.

It was a near thing getting up the stairs.

I just made it on to the jacks. I had the runs.

I leaned forward with my head in my hands.

And then I saw something.

It was jammed in behind the sink.

I pulled it out. It was a porno mag. Readers' wives. They were in bits. On their living-room sofas, legs spread. Arses in the air.

And something lit in me I hadn't felt in a long time.

And I wanted Helen that way.

I wanted to hurt her.

I wanted her to feel it and beg me to stop and beg me to go on.

So I pulled up my pants and I checked the rooms.

It was bright now.

In one room. Hamilton and Cliona Leeson were in bed together. I could see her tits. It spurred me on.

Sheila Shitebag was in the next room with a pillow over her face.

All I had to do was exert a little pressure.

But I had things on my mind.

I pushed Helen's door open slowly.

Sunlight streamed across her bed. I've never seen anything like it.

I wanted to shag her.

All those years I'd sat in my study reading the Elizabethans. I'd forgotten what those poems were about. They were foreplay. They were all about having it off.

I knelt on the bed.

And I couldn't do it.

I couldn't move. Reason had crept into the room behind me and caressed my neck.

This girl. I could only crave her attention, and ruin her.

I was thinking about my girl you see?

I was thinking about something real.

I got up quietly and I left.

The traffic was beginning to thicken.

The first of the commuters.

I was walking west.

Canterbury was in Kent. Where Chaucer sent his pilgrims. Where Christopher Marlowe was born. He was murdered in Kent too.

Wasn't much of that now.

I walked the whole morning.

Had to keep taking a rest.

It was getting hot.

I went up into Crystal Palace Park. Through the long avenues of trees, up to the ruins of Crystal Palace itself. I lay there in the sun and I closed my eyes.

I'd made a total fool of myself.

I couldn't understand how I'd been so stupid as to think anything would have come of this. And I'd fucked myself up as far as Dublin was concerned. Everywhere I went people would laugh. I must have looked like a lunatic.

I was bolloxed.

Chaucer's pilgrims went by.

Christopher Marlowe was arguing about the bill. My daughter climbed into bed beside me. And then someone pulled her out and I heard her screaming.

I woke up. It was dusk.

I was sweating booze.

I was thirsty. Miles from anywhere.

I had to get out of the park before it got too dark to see.

I scratched the gravel out of my hair stood up.

And as I did, I saw something move down by the steps. It was dark and huddled. I thought it was a big dog. I was frightened of dogs. I stood looking. I didn't want to provoke it by moving.

I was going to find another way out of the park. And then, suddenly, it stood up. It was a man.

He looked quite young. Thirty maybe. He started walking towards me.

For a second I thought I was going to be mugged, but there was something about him that made me comfortable.

It was relaxing to watch his easy stride. I just wanted to watch him walk.

As he got nearer I could see he was smiling.

'Beautiful night,' he said.

'Yes,' I said.

He stood beside me and we looked out over the lights of the city.

All those lives.

And then he said, 'Getting dark. We'd want to get back to civilisation.'

'That's a good idea,' I said.

And we began to stroll along.

It was like I'd known him for a long time.

It was natural for us to do this.

Down into the park. Very quiet.

'Were you asleep up there?' he asked me.

'I must have been,' I said, 'Rough night, last night.'

He laughed and said, 'I know what that's like.'

Then he offered me his hand and said,

'My name's William by the way.'

We shook hands. He was cool.

Not cold, like you'd expect a vampire to be.

He was just right. I think I wanted him to touch my face. I wasn't sure. It was getting hard to think. It was easier just to walk.

Interval.

Part Two

They have power. Not the power to make you do what they want.

But real power. To make you want what they want. It hurts to consider things in their company. It becomes hard to make sense. They appeal to the older part of us.

What we share with animals.

That's what they have you see.

So that when William hailed a taxi, I think I got in first.

I'm not sure how far we went.

We stopped on a wide suburban street. Old houses. Imposing pillars.

High trees.

I can still smell the house.

It was damp stones and running water and dry bark. It was familiar and exciting; I was sort of drifting you see.

The walls were panelled with dark wood. The carpets were a deep rich red.

An ornate banister.

We went into the kitchen.

It was warm and comfortable.

But there was something about it.

Took me a while to figure out what it was.

There was no food.

William put a bottle of Glenfiddich on the table and I took a good lash of it. He sat with me while I drank.

We didn't say anything.

It was quite dark, but I could see his eyes, bright, like a cat.

He seemed to be a bit embarrassed by it and he looked away.

I wanted to believe I was still dreaming.

I wanted to be afraid.

And then he said, 'Six of us live here. The others are women. We need someone like you. It's better if we don't go out. We prefer it if people come here to socialise. Nobody dies, we only take what we need, and they don't become like us. We have always been like this.

You can go to bars or clubs or wherever. Bring young people. There's a party here every night and you'll find they want to come with you. They leave unharmed and they never remember being here.'

'Can you only come out at night?' I said. He smiled and said it was more convenient for them to live at night, because people are more willing to have a nice time then. 'Is it a nice time?' I said.

He looked at me, his eyes pale, pale blue. 'It's a wonderful time,' he said.

And I believed him.

I was drunk. I was . . .

'Will you do it for me?' he said.

And I felt that saying no was like refusing a friend their dying wish. 'Of course I will,' I said.

And then I was very tired.

He brought me up the dark staircase to a door with more stairs and up into the attic. It was a low ceiling, a bed, a desk, a small window, a bathroom.

'You might like this,' he said.

I turned and saw him standing at a bookcase. Everything I'd need.

I touched them. And I saw a Bible. 'You don't mind this book?' I said.

He shook his head.

'Nature made us both,' he said, 'And I don't like garlic because it makes my breath smell. That's the only reason.'

'Superstition,' he said.

Then he frowned and sat on the bed.

'I'll tell you something strange, though,' he said.

'There's a tradition in eastern Europe. You can keep a vampire away from your house by sprinkling rice on your windowsill. The vampire is compelled to count every grain, and luckily he'll still be counting when the morning comes. And for some reason that's sort of true.'

I wasn't sure whether he was joking with me but he seemed to be serious.

He told me he had an overwhelming desire to know how many grains were in a pile. And he seemed to think there was something noble about that. Something that proved he had a deep sense of enquiry and not just a stupid obsession. Fucking rice . . .

That was the first sign I got of his vanity.

That he thought he was more than he was. He turned all his faults into virtues. But that night I was stupid enough and happy enough just to feel . . . ah!

He shook my hand and left the room. I sat at the desk and looked out at the tops of the trees.

And I found myself trying to miss my family. But something wouldn't let me.

I could only miss what they were like years ago.

And that's the way life is, you can't have that, can you?

You can't light a stranger's face with the mention of Santa.

You can only do that to certain people for a certain time.

And then nature makes everybody a cunt because one day you look around and you're all in each others' way.

Mm. There's always going to be a smugness about you listening to this.

As we all take part in this convention. And you will say, 'These vampires are not very believable, are they?'

And you are entitled.

This convention. These restrictions, these rules, they give us that freedom.

I have the freedom to tell you this unhindered, while you can sit there assured that no one is going to get hurt. Possibly offended, but you'll live. We're all quite safe here. Safe to say things like, 'If they were vampires, why don't their victims become vampires?' And you are, of course, relying on the lazy notions foisted upon you by others in the effort to make you buy more popcorn.

But when you find out that they are real, that all changes, you see.

Let's think about it, will we? For a moment. If a vampire bites you and you in turn become a vampire, that's a rule.

A causal, mechanical rule: 'Vampirism is deadly contagious.'

A rule that says their species, like ours, must survive. And that's natural, we suppose. And, that seems to make sense, fine. But we want it both ways.

We want the vampire's bite to be 'magic'. Death-defying, supernatural.

Why?

Why do we need it to be magic?

Because magic doesn't exist?

We don't have to be afraid of what doesn't exist.

Or is it because we envy them?

We're jealous of their power to instil fear in others.

And we can't have that, and if we can't, nothing can?

But we never seem to think for a moment that nature is magic.

We view nature scientifically. We can predict its laws.

But our pride in doing this blinds us. Blinds us to this simple fact: we don't know why there are laws at all.

We may know that the earth goes around the sun. And we may know that this is due to 'gravity'.

But not one of us knows why there is gravity. So don't sit there and cast judgement on the credibility of what I say, when you don't even know why you aren't floating off your seats.

I woke at the desk.

It was morning.

I could half remember hearing laughter during the night. Women.

It was another glorious day.

I had a wash and I went down.

The house was nowhere near as spooky in the bright. It was just dusty.

There was a note on the fridge. 'This is for you.' It was packed with food. There was food all over the place.

I went out the back. Sweet smell, rotten fruit.

I could just see the roofs of the houses on either side.

Just see them above the trees.

They needed repair.

And I knew no one lived there.

There were empty bottles all over the lawn and flies buzzed around the remains on the barbecue.

The sun was too much. I needed to be inside.

My wants were becoming very short term.

You see this was all part of it.

I spent the day reading up at my desk.

Drinking. A life of patronage. That's what I saw myself embarking upon.

Comfortable. I know.

Well.

I only noticed it was dusk when I heard movement downstairs.

Suddenly it was very cold.

There was a woman in the room.

She was black and her hair was dead straight.

She was sleek. Muscular.

I felt like I was floating backwards. That's the effect.

My spine melted into my belly and bubbled away there.

She held a bag out towards me.

I reached for it and she lightly scraped her nails over the back of my hand. And I was a baby wrapped up for the night. And then she was gone.

I sat there with my eyes half-closed. Waves of well-being rolling through me. The bag full of clothes. They were just the thing. Dashing. Dishevelled and dashing. They were me.

I could hear more activity.

Doors banging. A row. Someone laughing.

And then footsteps on the stairs.

William.

'Good evening,' he said. 'You look good in that.' Then he sat on the bed and said, 'Mmm, days of cloistered reflection. Reading. Thinking. Are you ready to go?'

'Those women,' I said.

'They won't bother you,' he said, 'They've been warned. Most beautiful women you'll ever see. But fall under their care, you'll wish you were dead, believe me.'

Then he said I should get going.

'I don't know if I'm the social type,' I said. He grinned at me.

'I think you'll find you are,' he said.

He put some money on the desk and then he left.

I stood there, the light fading.

It was time to go. And . . . I suddenly felt . . . light on my feet. Energetic. I wanted to go out.

I went down. I didn't see anyone but it was like I could feel the anticipation. The house. The house had it.

Out on the road I was wondering which way to go, and a taxi just pulled up without me hailing it. I could feel that things were different. I was in it.

I was weak.

'Take me into town,' I said.

That first night I did it.

I walked down into Leicester Square. The tourists and the ticket touts. How the living fuck I was going to invite anyone back to a party was quite fucking beyond me. As was why I was doing this. But Christ knows we all like to be busy. And. It's easy, when you're told what to do. When the choices narrow. When you're under authority. That's why there's so many madcap schemes and bad artists.

And why journalists wank so much, ah?

There's no excuse.

I went into a pub.

Everybody was standing.

I had a drink. I was looking around.

People finished work. Young people, with that shine off them.

This was ridiculous.

But then, suddenly, it wasn't the slightest bit ridiculous.

A young woman was at my elbow trying to get a round.

She was a blondy little thing with a pixie face.

'Excuse me,' I said, and I moved sideways to let her get to the bar.

'Thanks,' she said, 'What'll you have? It's my birthday.'

And I knew. I knew I'd been filled with charm. I'd been made attractive.

This was the gift I'd been given to bring people back.

'Your birthday!' I said, 'Please, allow me.'

'No,' she said, 'I couldn't, I'm with a group.'

I looked around. They were perfect.

Twenties. Good-looking. Lots of energy. 'I'll have a pint, then,' I said.

Her name was Dominique.

She worked for a magazine.

The people she was with were college friends. From Oxford.

She invited me to join them. Which I duly did.

And duly got bolloxed out of my fucking face. And held them enthralled with my brutal wit. We looked like a bunch of saps and their rich daddy, I think. We were a tidy half-dozen. At closing time we went for a pizza and wine, and more wine.

The stupid evening ablaze with drink and bullshit.

And then I had an 'idea'.

'Let's all go back to my house, for God's sake!' And I have to admit it. I was curious. I didn't like them. I was looking forward to seeing what was going to happen to them. I think you'd call that, having a streak in you.

And naturally by this time, we're inseparable and we pile into taxis.

All dry wit and our best clothes.

Chugging through the lights into the suburbs.

Down the dark road to William's house.

Music was drifting around from the back garden.

I led them down the side passage.

And I shut the gate.

There were candles lit all around the garden.

But there was no one there.

Tables were laid with drink.

We sat on stone benches.

I slugged on a bottle of wine.

But it was more than just being drunk in that place. It was like drowning. Gulping water for air and not being able to stop.

The youngsters fell around, dancing. In each others' arms.

And then, gradually, I noticed that there were more people. Moving among them.

The women. Jesus Christ. Heart-breakingly beautiful women.

You could see them and you couldn't.

Just like beauty in real life.

Sometimes it's there, and sometimes it should be. And it's not.

And after a while, I could feel the air. It began to fizz with pointless regret. And slowly, in twos and threes, they began to lie down in the grass.

And the moon and stars were shining down on this, and it was just another one of the things that goes on.

Nothing special.

I went to bed.

I woke up about ten.

Only the faintest twinge of a hangover. I'd gotten off lightly.

I went downstairs for some water, and there at the kitchen table, slumped over was Dominique.

I woke her. She was weak and she had a headache but that was all. I mean, fuck, I gave her some paracetamol, you know? I mean . . .

She couldn't remember anything about the party.

We went around waking her friends.

They were all over the place, on the floor, on the grass, one was even in a fucking hedge. I got them up.

Dominique gave me a kiss. I grabbed her hand. And they were happy, you know? They talked about getting a cure.

I saw them out. No harm done. I tidied up a bit. It was okay. Doing this. Being this thing.

I did it again the next night, and the one after. And after that. And that's how the next while was.

Flirting in bars. Getting . . . affection.

Back for a party. Getting them out in the morning. Everyone happy to be there and happy to leave.

Every time I did it, it was going to be the last time, but . . .

I'd think about the reception I'd get back in Dublin, and I wasn't up to it. I'd give it a few more days.

And . . . I'd keep giving it a few more days. I stayed away from the vampires, as much as I could.

The only one I spoke to was William. But I'd wish he'd leave me alone.

I'd be in the attic, and I'd read, and . . . I even began to do a little bit of writing. It was coming a bit easier, you see, because there were no knackers like me around the place who were going to tear it apart. It was just small things, things I'd remember. But I'll be straight with you. It wasn't very good.

And I'd be doing this you see and William would come to visit me.

I didn't want him to.

There was something.

He looked like us. But. He wasn't a human. And I had to think to work out what made him different.

And it was hard to think in that place. But I made the effort and I worked it out. How he was different from us. And it showed me what we are. What it is that makes us what we are.

But it took a good while.

I was curious about them of course. I began to have a look at them, sleeping. Sometimes they were all in the one bed. And sometimes I couldn't find them.

But they slept just like us.

And they'd wake up if I made a noise. Once, one of the women opened her eyes and I immediately got weak.

Weak in here. Took everything just to get back to my room.

And I had to lie down.

I stopped checking on them.

There was a gap.

And so, there I'd be, trying to write something. Trying to capture the care I once had, you see. My kids on Christmas Eve. Something like that.

And I'd feel him come in.

And of all things, he'd talk about art. And advise me about writing.

It was always the same.

The art object is different from every other object, he said, because it's not for anything.

A chair only is what it is because it's for sitting on. A knife only is what it is because it's for cutting.

But art is for itself.

Just as goodness is. It's for its own sake. Art is like having a go at making virtue. And he'd criticise me for my fear.

Fear of my work not being 'good' enough. The act itself is good, he said. You see how cerebral he was, nothing else. And I could never stand a pep talk. All that glib psychoanalytic wank.

So one day I got annoyed and said it must be brilliant living for so long, gathering all this wisdom.

He didn't say anything for a while. He looked a bit shook. And then in his true, corny, way. He told me a story.

A, Jesus, a fucking, story.

He told me there was a man where he came from, a long time ago.

And he was a woodsman.

And he was one of the happiest men who ever lived. Because he had married a woman who he loved more than himself.

His heart swelled at the thought of her. She was present to him at every moment of his lonely day out in the woods.

His only disappointment in life was that they couldn't have children.

Their innocence.

But it wasn't to be and he accepted his lot.

And that's what this man's life was like. And one day he was working out in the woods. And he heard someone crying. It was a strange sound. Near and far away at the same time. He dropped his axe and he went towards it. He called out and he was guided by the cries. And he saw why the sound was so strange. In the woods was a well and the crying came from the well.

He looked down, and in the water far below was an old man desperately clinging to the bucket, trying to stay afloat.

So the woodsman worked and strained and pulled him out. And then lay him down to recover. But it was too late. The old man was dying.

With his last breaths, he thanked the woodsman for his kindness and told him to look in his satchel. And in the satchel were tools for watchmaking. And there was a new watch. The most beautiful watch the woodsman had ever seen.

The old man told the woodsman that he wanted him to keep it.

It could tell more than just the time he said. And then he died.

And it wasn't until many years later that the woodsman found out what the watch's secret was. He was out in the woods one winter's day and it was getting dark.

He looked at the watch but it had stopped.

He tried winding it but it didn't seem to work. But then he wound it backwards and something changed.

The light. Somehow it had become brighter. The sun was higher in the sky.

He wound it back another hour and the sun rose higher.

He could travel in time.

He wound it forward again and the sun went down.

Understandably he was a bit fucking amazed.

You see, this is the art of understatement. And he never told anyone about it, not even his beloved wife.

It was a secret.

And being an honest fellow, he never saw what practical use such a thing could have. He never used it to travel.

He wasn't interested. Everything he loved was in the present.

That was, until his wife died.

And the woodsman was heartbroken.

And naturally he couldn't resist going back a little, now and then, to hold her once again. And his infatuation never ceased.

He was fascinated by her.

He was in love, do you see?

And he began to go back a little further. Until it got to the stage where he went back further than he'd ever gone.

To see her as a child, before he had known her.

He was an old man watching this child play.

But this only made him feel his loss even more. He knew his time with her was over.

He faced up to it and decided he must live alone until he saw her again in heaven.

But he found that the watch was now truly broken and would not wind at all.

He was stuck in the past.

Where nobody knew him. Not even his wife, since she was just a little girl.

But she was all he had. He panicked.

Terror. He took the child.

He picked her up and ran into the woods with her in his frail arms.

And she was crying and screaming.

And he couldn't let her go.

And then he was tired and he couldn't go any further. And they fell together in the leaves. And he held on to her. You know?

And the townspeople caught him and beat him.

And left him.

When William finished telling me this we were . . . very quiet.

And then I asked him, what does it mean? And he didn't know.

He looked a bit bewildered. And then he laughed and fucked off.

He didn't know what his story meant.

He knew he was supposed to be informed by it but it was just a story that he told.

A story about not being able to get back.

And that was all.

And that's what makes us different.

We reflect.

They don't.

They see what they want. They get it.

Do anything to get it.

William couldn't hold a child any more than, than you or I could push a glass of water away when we're parched.

And I think he wanted . . .

That was the horror of the whole thing.

The cunt wanted a conscience.

He fucking regretted not being able to regret the things he did.

And when I realised this, he began to disgust me.

Clinging to all this human bollocks, lecturing me on what was wrong with my life.

This unreflective animal. Christ.

All his foibles. His virtues. For fuck's sake. Man was a butcher. Slept all day.

Came out and bit people. Fucking knacker.

So it came to . . .

We were in the kitchen one evening before I went out for some youngsters.

And to be honest with you, as usual, I was a bit pissed.

There we were, leaning on the worktop, all philosophical. All ordinary.

How the world had fucked me up and this was where I belonged.

Where there were no great expectations of me. Where I could relax.

You know? Like he knew anything beyond how hungry he felt.

And this, the immorality of what I'd been doing over the last few years.

Jesus, I knew that!

If I didn't I wouldn't have had a problem.

I knew what I'd been doing was wrong.

That's why I did it.

I enjoyed the looks of fear and hatred I'd gotten whenever I went into an actors' pub.

I behaved that way, because it was wrong. But William had no because.

He couldn't buck nature.

He had no choice the way a dog has no choice.

Reasons don't come into it.

And there he was talking to me about the autonomy of the art object and things like this.

It was sad. It was boring.

And these vampire bitches moving through the house. Brushing by.

These . . . things men would die for.

Getting in here. Bringing every whim you've got firmly down into your pants.

I can't overstate their power to distract.

I was all confused whenever they came near me.

And William knew this. You know?

He'd let them be around, so I couldn't think straight.

So he could have the floor.

Fuck. He was welcome to it.

I had nothing to say to him.

I just thought, 'Ah, Jesus, would you just . . . '

You know?

And I grabbed this jar of rice and I smashed it on the floor.

William was a bit startled at first, but then, suddenly, I was just another object in the room. And him, and I think two others . . . got down on the floor and started to count. I thought I better get going.

William was saying, 'Wait, come, come back.'

But he was lost in the rice.

And I had a moment of clarity.

No more messing . . .

This was the last night I was doing this. This was the last batch of idiots I was bringing back.

And after that . . . Well I didn't know. I'd see.

I took a cab into Soho.

A bar with a late licence.

I sat there for a few hours and it began to fill up as all the other bars closed.

It was a kip, and I had to be the oldest codger in the place.

But the old charm was there and pretty soon I was getting greeted. And smiled at. Who did they think I was, for fuck's sake? And I was at the bar with this group of rich kids.

Exchanging stories about the old days that are all gone now.

Oh yeah, I knew them all. Name them. I knew them. He was a drinker. Let me tell you. Let me tell you. Mmm.

What are we doing here? I know somewhere we can go. Yeah.

I think I was aware of her before I saw her.

The first thing I saw was her feet.

Bare feet in open sandals.

The sinews in her ankle shifting with her weight.

Helen.

She was looking at me.

These people were actors.

She had every right to stare at me.

What I'd done.

And as far as anyone knew, from Dublin, I had disappeared.

And here I was regaling the young things in London.

I looked her in the eye.

I could feel the tears coming.

Made me annoyed.

I was embarrassed.

I wanted to kill everybody. Get out.

But I'd forgotten the charm, hadn't I?

She leaned forward and kissed me.

I could have anything I wanted.

'People have been wondering about you,' she said.

'People . . . Let me get you a drink,' I said. And I bought a round.

You see this was the first time I'd been surrounded by artists and actually felt in charge.

This was the ideal last batch.

In the morning, none of them would remember what had happened.

And I would know.

And they'd be fools in my eyes for ever. I had power now.

But Helen.

This could be different in her case. In our case.

I could keep her away from the others.

Bring her up to the attic. Lock the door.

And she'd be . . .

She'd want to lie down with me.

Until it got bright.

And a big clock would go back, and when we woke up, how the world would have changed. That was my wish.

'Let's go,' I said.

'Come on,' and we piled into cabs. And for the second time in as many months she was beside me.

Her cool body.

A soothing fucking you know? A . . .

And all the others were drunk as maniacs.

I leaned into her.

'You've got to stay beside me tonight,' I said. She didn't even question it. I was beginning to miss things.

The spell was breaking.

Human company.

We got to the house.

Probably the most people I'd ever brought back.

I held her hand.

And I led everybody around the back.

And I got a shock.

The vampires were there already.

All around the garden.

Quiet. Watching us. No music tonight. The young actors didn't care.

They were caught up in the easy confusion of the place. Ten times as drunk as when they'd left the bar.

And the worst thing.

William was only looking at me.

He was annoyed at me.

I'd let him down.

He'd been all clever one minute and the next he was down on the floor counting rice.

I'd reminded him what he was and what he wasn't.

The women didn't waste any time.

Already there were tangles of limbs.

And William was just looking at me.

I took Helen into the house.

She was nodding off.

I had to get her out.

I began to panic.

As much as one can panic when every thought is like looking for something in . . . tar. We went into the hall.

And one of the women was on the stairs.

I couldn't move.

I couldn't feel Helen.

She was gone.

The woman came towards me.

I was in for it.

My legs began to wobble.

She took me in her arms and lifted me. Dancing slowly in the hall.

We were up the banister, we were down in a corner. We were drifting.

The joy of submitting to something like that.

To put yourself in someone's care.

Trust has nothing to do with it.

It's abandon.

And then the stupid cow bit me.

And it fucking hurt.

My arm was getting cold.

I passed out.

And then, thump, we were on the ground. I could feel my weight again.

I was a fat bastard on the floor.

The woman was on top of me.

She was dozy.

There was blood all down my shirt. Down my pants.

Only consolation I had was she might get a hangover that'd knock her off her feet for days. She'd bitten the wrong fellow. It would have been nice to lie there for a while. But the alarm bells were ringing. I had to find Helen.

Fuck. I couldn't believe I'd been bitten. I went back out to the garden.

Dawn was coming. The vampires were gone in. People lay about.

Helen wasn't there.

She wasn't in the kitchen or the lounge. She wasn't on the stairs.

Then I heard talking.

It was in the attic.

It was William.

His sing-song.

His lilt.

I crept up. Slowly.

He was talking about me.

About the world and how it had spoiled me.

Ah, he was spoofing.

Pretending he could think.

I got to the door.

Helen was on my bed.

She had hardly any clothes on.

She'd been bitten too.

And William was sitting beside her.

Talking rubbish.

The epitome of nature's thoughtlessness.

The desire to survive.

That's all he was.

But he didn't know that.

And looking at the two of them there. No comparison.

She was so beautiful.

And he was a black-looking thing that was hardly even there.

And I was more her than him. A good feeling.

And I just said, 'Leave her alone you smelly prick.'

He looked up at me, and I swear to God, his eyes were blazing red. I'm not joking. But, because of that, the situation didn't seem very real. And I wasn't scared. 'Helen,' I said, 'Get up.'

She obeyed me the way a sick child does.

Slowly, with resignation.

'Do you want me to leave?' he said. 'No, stay there,' I said, 'I'm going.'

He looked at the bookcase for a moment, and then he said, 'You won't be happy.'

'Probably not,' I said, 'But it wouldn't be much fun if I was.' Know what I mean?

Then I put my arm around Helen and brought her down the stairs.

He didn't follow us and I don't why he let me go.

Maybe wanting a conscience is the same as having one.

Because it's all the same effort, isn't it? Maybe he was just imitating us.

I lay Helen on a couch with one of her pals. She slept. I gave her a kiss, and then I left them to their hangovers.

The summer was fading.

There was a chill in the morning.

I walked down the street and I thought about the fuss people were going to make of me.

The potential it gave me to bully sympathy out of everybody.

Back from my breakdown.

On the right track again, yeah?

I'd 'Embrace My Second Chance.'

I'd do a piece about 'Getting Back.'

Getting back in touch with things.

Talking To My Wife.

Giving My Children My Advice.

I had my health.

I had resolve.

But most important.

Over everything else.

I had a story.

So, were they real?

Or were they a dream?

Well, I've got to ask you, what the hell isn't a dream?

Your projections for the future. Your fantasies.

Your fears. Your rude awakenings.

What the hell is that if it's not any night's sleep?

And that person you fell head over heels for.

What the hell was that?

What was the moment it hit you?

Love, Christ. If it was love at first sight, what the hell you doing giving some stranger the benefit of the doubt?

Entrusting them with everything you've got?

Because of what you wanted them to be?

Well, that's a dream-life if ever there was one,

And if it wasn't love at first sight, and it was a gradual thing.

Like a wound healing.

Let me ask you this: don't you begin to resent that person in equal amounts? For sneaking up on you, and denying you all the chaotic excitement you felt your love should have been?

And if neither of these are true for you and you're in the middle of it, and you haven't fucking blown it yet. And you're the happiest person in the room . . .

Well, your presence blesses everyone else here, doesn't it? Because you're the embodiment of hope, aren't you? You're hope incarnate.

Where are you? Where are you?

Where?

Afterword

Rum and Vodka
November 1992

Rum and Vodka premiered in November 1992 at University College Dublin where I was completing an MA in Philosophy. I wrote the play when I was twenty. It was the first monologue I wrote. Up until then I'd been doing normal ensemble plays with lots of characters talking to each other endlessly. These plays were written with perhaps a sense of wanting to be a playwright rather than wanting to be a good writer. But *Rum and Vodka* is the play with which I think I found my voice.

I directed a student friend, Stephen Walshe, in the first production. He was a commerce student with a great interest in theatre. It never occurred to me that a full-length monologue might be difficult for an actor to learn. I just thought it would be like telling a long joke. You don't have to be word-perfect as long as people are getting the gist. Of course this was bullshit. If you forget your lines, it's a nightmare. Someone who was being so lucid a minute ago is suddenly stammering like a terrified donkey.

Some time later Brian Cox dried in a production of my monologue, *St Nicholas*, in London. Years of experience gave him the confidence to merely turn to the crowd and say, 'I'm terribly sorry, ladies and gentlemen, I wonder would you mind very much if I started again?' As he was only about six minutes in, nobody seemed to care, in fact many people said they found it very exciting to have this happen. However, one woman reviewing the play for BBC radio did complain about this mishap, as though Brian was an athlete who was expected to perform like an automaton. Live theatre always has the possibility of turning into a mess, and that's part of it. That's part of the fun.

But back to *Rum and Vodka*. Stephen Walshe had a photographic memory. He told me he could literally see the page in front of him as he spoke to the audience. He was 'reading' it.

Lots of people came to see it and we had a good time. So when the opportunity arose to do the play again for a week at Trinity

College in the centre of Dublin, we jumped at the chance. But there was a slight problem. The week we were given was right before the summer exams, so we were playing to literally nobody. One night only one young woman showed up, and she didn't seem to have great English. My friend, Colin O'Connor, and I went up to the dressing room to tell Stephen we were pulling the show. But Stephen said he wanted to do it. Colin and I were having the same thought: giving a long monologue to one foreign person was a bit weird and embarrassing. But Stephen wanted to do it. Finally we persuaded him that it was a much better idea to go and get drunk instead. I went to tell the foreign girl that the show was off. She too seemed quite disappointed, and she wandered off on her own. I still feel a bit stupid that I never invited her to come with us. But that might have been even weirder, sitting there in the pub explaining the play to her.

About a year later, some ex-students offered us a week to do *Rum and Vodka* in the basement of a café on Dublin's Quays. Again Stephen was mad eager to do it. This was a smelly little place and the 'lighting cues' consisted of switching the light on and off just like you would at home. Considering the bad language in the play I never wanted anyone watching the play who was too young. But one night, to my horror, I saw a ten-year-old kid sitting in the audience. I went and complained to the people at the door, but their argument was that they'd managed to charge him a full-price ticket.

The next production of the play was at the City Arts Centre, directed by Colin O'Connor. Everything was going quite well until the day of the artistic director's wedding, when some arsehole nicked the costume to wear to the do. Again it was a case of pulling the show for that evening. Oh well. Pub? Any excuse.

The Good Thief
April 1994

The Good Thief was first performed by an actor friend, Kevin Hely, under the title *The Light of Jesus*. We did it in a real theatre in Dublin, which cost us a fortune because nobody came. We did get some great reviews but no one knew who we were and the title was so off-putting. We hired slide projectors and displayed slides all the way through the show. These changed like any technical cue – when Kevin said a certain line we'd click one or other of the projectors, displaying something relevant to the narrative. Some pictures were fairly literal and others were ironic. And it was a pretty cool effect. The only drawback was that if Kevin made a mistake or lost his place in the story, the slides would be out of synch. They were loaded into the projectors in such a way that we'd never really have time to change the order they came in. At this time, Kevin, a Fly by Night member since the beginning, was holding down a job teaching computer science. He was also shooting a no-budget feature film in which he was playing the lead. In other words, he was knackered. We decided to open the show without any previews so we could be reviewed as soon as possible, gambling that we'd get critically acclaimed and sell out instantly. Ha ha.

What this practically meant was that we never gave Kevin a chance to publicly perform a full-length monologue before opening night.

He fainted onstage.

Everything was going fine until about half an hour in. I suddenly sensed that Kevin was about to forget his lines. It's weird with actors, you just know that they're going to 'dry' before it happens. You just think to yourself, 'You're gone. I can see it. You know about the next two lines, and then it's the abyss.' Kevin simply stopped talking and wandered over to the side of the stage where he sank to the floor and leaned against a pillar. Now had either of us been more experienced, I would have shouted his next line at him. But we felt, I suppose, that a loud prompt would ruin 'the illusion' we pretentiously thought we were creating. So I sat there beside one of the slide projectionists, Jason Byrne, and just gripped his arm. Years later he said he could still feel me nearly breaking his bones with terror. It seemed like minutes before Kevin started talking again – it was in fact a few seconds. The weird thing was, after the show people said they didn't remember this happening, or they just thought it was part of the play.

We performed to thin houses for two weeks and finished up losing whatever money we'd put in. And that should have been that. But there was an amount of enthusiasm from people asking us to give it another go somewhere else. And believe it or not, a theatre critic (!) set up a proper showcase for us at the Project Arts Centre. His name was Mic Moroney. He invited lots of journalist pals and people who worked in the proper theatre. Among them was a cousin of mine, Garrett Keogh, a professional actor who was well known in Ireland at the time because he was playing a villain in a soap opera called *Fair City*. He suggested to me that he perform the play, with me directing, and that we do it in the Dublin Theatre Festival.

I agreed and Garrett found a co-producer: self-styled Dublin film editor, Se Merry Doyle. Se and Garrett had been friends for many years. Se loved the play and it was decided that they'd produce it in a new student-union building in Temple Bar. As a venue it was designed for kids to drink and dance, i.e., it was a concrete bunker. Se and Garrett decided This Is Going To Be An Event. Opening a theatre where there hadn't been one before. This was really exciting. I was twenty-three and all this mad stuff was happening. New slide photography was commissioned. Entire banks of seats were built. A set designer was hired. The Abbey Theatre's lighting man was called in. I'd never done anything on this scale. My job was to help Garrett prepare for his role. This would be easy. Working with good actors is never very hard.

One day, walking down to the theatre, Garrett said, 'You know no one is going to come and see a play called *The Light of Jesus*, don't you?' 'Fuck them,' I replied, all flushed and idealistic. All theatrical. We walked a little further in silence, down past Bewley's on Westmoreland Street. Then Garrett turned to me with a strange mixture of concern and amusement, 'Do you know you're on ten per cent of the box-office takings?' I had a little think, which led to a little mumble, 'Well . . . I . . . had thought before about calling it . . . *The . . . Good Thief.*'

'Perfect,' said Garrett.

By the time we opened Garrett and Se had managed to create a bit of buzz. There was a wine reception. Frank McGuinness formally opened the 'theatre'. In the programme was a letter of congratulations from the Minister of Arts. Boozy journalists stared dourly at the proceedings. I stood joking with relatives and friends. Very nervous. When the play started, I stayed behind the audience, listening. And as soon as I knew there weren't going to be any disasters I went and stood at the bar with the chap who ran the building.

Some reviews were spectacular. And some were fairly shitty. The run never really took off. Some nights were three-quarters full, some were almost empty. Money was lost. Tensions began to generate. Garrett and Se finally fell out over a missing lens cap for a pair of binoculars one had borrowed from the other. Many nights during the run I slipped around to the Festival club for a late drink. One night I made a point of thanking a critic profusely for giving us a scathing review. He wasn't sure if I was making a mistake but couldn't bring himself to correct me. He was in agony. Meanwhile, our slide projectionist, Jason Byrne, got into a row with another unfavourable critic. We were toughening up. And when the run farted to an undistinguished close, I again thought, 'Well, that's the end of that.'

But a few weeks later, Garrett had come up with a surefire moneymaker, a national tour. The Arts Council in Ireland gives rural venues money to pay for touring productions to come and visit. Once the venue decides they'd like you to perform, they give you a guaranteed payment, even if no audience turns up. So we went back into rehearsals and slimmed the whole thing down. No more slide-projection nonsense. All we needed was a chair, and the tour began.

I went to see it in a couple of places and my most memorable time was at the Playhouse in Derry.

Garrett always had a whiskey bottle onstage while he performed and drank from it regularly. It contained apple juice. It looked like whiskey and it was easy to drink. But when we arrived in Derry our stage manager, Philip, couldn't find any apple juice in the shops. Garrett said he had to drink something. The show was starting in like ten minutes. We thought about what might work. Cold tea? No, disgusting. Red lemonade? No, too much fizz. What then? Garrett sighed and reached into his pocket. He handed me a ten. 'Get me a bottle of whiskey,' he said. And I did.

When I handed it to him he went to open it. 'No,' I said, 'Open it on stage in front of the audience. Let them hear the seal break. Let them know it's real.' And that's what happened. He opened it on stage and the mad bastard drank about half the bottle. Was he pissed? Well, let's just say there were a right few pauses towards the end of the show. But he did it and it was fine. Afterwards, me and Garrett and Philip polished the bottle off in the dressing room and then we went to the pub. As usual I got stuck talking to some headcheese. Garrett was talking to an ex-UVF prisoner and getting on great. At closing time we went into a pizza takeaway place where Half-Bottle-Of-Whiskey-Boy bought about ten pizzas for these middle-aged women he was suddenly best friends with. He was flying. Outside I was trying to persuade him not to get into a taxi with them. He had a show to do in Monaghan the next evening. But he knew best. And off he went.

Dr Jekyll met Mr Hyde in the morning. Garrett was a pale, shivering imitation of the man he used to be. It turned out that he'd gone back to a house in Derry's Republican stronghold, the Bogside. He'd been sitting there drinking with these women, thinking he was getting on fairly well, when there was a bang at the door. And in came four big lads in leather jackets. It was three o'clock in the morning and Garrett was there with their girlfriends. Considering both the hour and where they were, saying these men probably knew how to handle themselves had to be something of an understatement. So what did Garrett do? Did he behave himself? Did he ingratiate himself? Explain himself?

The way he told me, his thought process was this: 'This could be a bad situation. Something must be done to make sure it isn't. The best thing to do is take control. I'll be preemptive and confuse them.' So without a word being said, he leapt up and threw a few kung fu moves at them. Now, like a lot of people who pull stunts like this, Garrett didn't know kung fu. And it was probably lucky for him that he didn't. Because the lads never moved. They just stood there for a moment and then they started laughing at him and gave him a beer. This goes to show something. I don't know what though. It's often hard to learn from a true original.

So that morning we set out to drive to Monaghan. Bruce Lee decided he should lie in the back of the car and sleep for the journey. But he was still a bit off his face, chatting away and telling us jokes and stories and spoofs. And every time Boyzone came on the radio singing 'Love Me for a Reason', Garrett goes, 'There's your song, Conor.' In Monaghan we got Garrett some food. He ate some steak and chips and then finally went for a snooze in the car.

It turned out that I was going to be operating the lights for the show, which was a fairly simple task. They came up at the beginning and went down at the end. Poor Garrett struggled gamely on. I'm being unfair. He was great. Until the last line. All along, during the run in Dublin, during the tour, his performance had been downbeat, subtle, he wasn't hitting everybody over the head with what he was saying, nor was he patronisingly leading them by the hand. But in Monaghan, in his weakened state and with diminished judgement, he decided to give the last line a little bit of quivering emotion. Just as he said, 'I was trying to get out of the rain,' he let his voice break. The tiniest sob, but enough. Enough to make me think, 'What the fuck are you playing at?' And instead of bringing the lights down on his last line I left them at full power, leaving Garrett standing there with no more lines. Just standing there waiting for the blackout. Until I began the slowest fade, thinking, 'Act now, you fucker . . .' Cruel, no?

This Lime Tree Bower
September 1995

Casting *Lime Tree Bower* was a new experience for me. Many of my friends from the Fly by Night Theatre Company were unavailable either because they had travelled abroad or they were being formally trained as actors at Trinity College. Trinity didn't allow their students to act in productions outside the course. So for the first time I had to actually get in touch with agents and say, 'Send me actors to audition.' And they did. Auditioning is something you need a bit of a technique for. You want to seem friendly, but not get anyone's hopes up too much. I usually decide in the first few minutes if someone can (a) Act and (b) Play the part. You know in the first few seconds when someone's wrong. But out of courtesy you give them the full twenty minutes or whatever.

I saw a few good people but the final decisions were relatively easy. I had already offered the part of the lecturer, Ray, to a Dublin actor, Conor Mullen. I'd seen him in a play at the Peacock and immediately knew he'd be brilliant. I accosted him in the pub across the road and met him a few days later when he'd read the script. One of the best decisions I've made. (If you ever get connected to the Irish telephone automated-information system, it's Conor's voice you'll hear. Listen to the authority.)

The parts of Joe and Frank went to Ian Cregg and Niall Shanahan, respectively, two actors I found through audition. It's always incredible how the people who are right for the part just seem to appear ready-made. You think, 'What the hell am I going to do for the next few weeks? They don't need me to tell them anything much.' But it's about confidence. You spend time telling them they can do it. They should do it. This is the only thing they should ever do. And the fools buy it.

Because they all deliver monologues, I was working with them separately. They didn't see each other from the first readthrough until the final week of rehearsal. They'd ask me, 'How are the others getting on?' And I'd say, 'Okay. Not as good as you.' When they finally met to rehearse the whole thing together they nearly jumped on each other with relief that they were all in the same boat. They were a great cast and a good bunch to have fun with.

We were playing in the Fringe Festival and the show was an immediate smash. We sold out every night. The cast was on profit-share, and almost unbelievably for a fringe show, they got paid at the end. It wasn't much, considering they'd rehearsed for free too, but I was delighted there was no bad taste in anyone's mouth. In fact things got better.

At this time I was pretty much unemployed. I was writing but it wasn't paying. But a literary agent from London, Nick Marston, came to see *Lime Tree* and took me on, saying he felt theatres in London would be dying to stage it. This was cool, walking around saying things like, 'Yeah, that's a pain in the ass. Actually, I was just saying to my agent in London, the other day . . . '

Within a fortnight offers to meet theatre bosses in London were coming through. I flew over. And there I was riding around on the Tube between the Royal Court in Sloane Square and the Bush in Shepherd's Bush. And, in between, meeting my publisher. *Meeting my publisher!*

I suppose the start of good things is the best time. I remember that day very clearly. I knew I had come to some corner. I knew I could go back, but I didn't want to.

I decided to do the play at the Bush because they had no quibbles with me bringing the Dublin cast over. We came to London the following summer straight into blistering heat and pollution. Me and Niall Shanahan had terrible hay fever. We were all staying in different places for the first while. Ian was sleeping on someone's landing. Niall had a room in a house but there was no door in the frame.

The Bush Theatre is a hundred-seater above a pub. After rehearsals we sat in the pub and went for Indian takeaways. And earlier in the year the Bush had asked me to become their writer-in-residence, which meant they paid me some money. I was also getting paid because my screenplay, *I Went Down*, was going into production. This felt nuts.

I remember me and Conor Mullen staying in digs near Stamford Brook. It was a house owned by a semi-retired actress, Sheila Burnette. She was very kind to us. There were strict rules, but once you obeyed them there were no problems. A very tranquil memory I have is waking up in blazing sunshine. My room faced the back garden. We had been out on the batter the night before. I could hear voices chatting away merrily outside. Down in the garden, stretched out on deck chairs, were Conor and Sheila sipping mid-morning gin and tonics, watching the planes landing and taking off from Heathrow. These two people just commenting on the planes in the sunshine. One of those moments when you think, that's the pace we should strive for.

Towards the end of rehearsals the lads were finally given a house they could share. It was a nice place, small, terraced, with a conservatory at the back. There were two proper bedrooms and a half-converted attic with a ladder going up into it. Niall Shanahan always considered himself the unluckiest member of the cast. There was no reason why he should have been. He just seemed to project a kind of resignation. When the three boys came to draw lots for the rooms, he didn't even bother. He knew he'd get the attic. And he did.

Conor Mullen got the big bedroom. He was the opposite of Niall. He also had the most comfortable chair onstage. He didn't fight for it or anything. Conor just *seemed* right in that chair. It's hard to describe. They were all lovely blokes. They just had different levels of confidence. It was a fascinating dynamic. It was funny. Niall just felt like he deserved the worst room, the worst chair, the hottest costume.

But as soon as they started acting, they were completely their characters. Especially in London. Niall was unsettlingly confident as Frank. And Conor gave us intriguing glimpses of the insecurity behind Ray's brash, bullying exterior.

The first preview came along. I was certain it was going to be a disaster. I couldn't believe we'd made it that far and I still can't believe that Ian Cregg got up and started the play in front of a strange audience. I was like, 'What's wrong with these people? How the hell are we getting away with this?' But we were and we did.

My dad and my two sisters had travelled over from Dublin to be with me for the opening. When I met up with them before the first show, they had decided to take a taxi from their hotel to Shepherd's Bush right in the middle of rush hour. The trip had cost them something like fifty pounds. I was furious. I felt responsible. They didn't know London. I was the reason they were here. They were by no means wealthy and here they were getting ripped off, paying ten times what they'd have had to on the Tube. And horribly, they didn't care as long as they could be with me for this important night. Somehow I knew things had changed. The stakes were all higher now. If things went well, the rewards and opportunities would be great. If not, you were staring down a well of disappointment you could visit and draw from as much as you liked. And no one would bother you.

But the reviews were all great. Part of the satisfaction I drew from this, besides making some money and generally having a success, was the attention the actors were getting from high-powered agencies like ICM and PFD. Film and TV producers were coming to check them out with offers of auditions and screen tests for various projects. No longer were they sitting in the house or wandering around London before the show. They were reading scripts and going to meetings. Brilliant.

St Nicholas
February 1997

St Nicholas was the play I wrote for the Bush as their writer-in-residence. It was a one-man play for a man in his fifties. I was to direct. I had long chats with the new artistic director, Mike Bradwell, about who should play it. It was difficult to know. We knew it needed someone with a strong presence who could give us bleak devastation and make it funny. I suggested that I'd had Brian Cox in mind when I wrote it. I'd even cut his picture out of a magazine and stuck it on the folder I was using for the play. As far as I was concerned this was wishful thinking. He was so busy doing films, and how could you persuade an Olivier Award-winning actor to come to a pub and work for two hundred quid a week? Mike mulled it over and said, 'I don't know. Let's send it to him. Brian's just about mad enough to do it.'

So off the script went. To Hollywood. A few days later the phone rang: 'Conor? This is Brian Cox. I want to give you my dates to see if we can work something out.' I couldn't accept that this was happening so smoothly. I went out for a long walk. I walked for hours down on the beach in Dollymount. I got in after dark. A grinning idiot.

Given Brian's busy schedule we broke the rehearsal period up. One week on, two weeks off, another week, another break, and two weeks before opening. Consequently we rehearsed in a number of different places.

The first was Riverside Studios in Hammersmith. I didn't know Brian. I was nervous. He was very enthusiastic and put me at ease in rehearsal. We drank a lot of tea. This first week was quite lonely. I was in a town I didn't know very well and there wasn't a full cast to associate with. We had to rely on each other.

The weather was freezing, it was the first week in January and night fell at five o'clock. I'd sort of make my way half-heartedly back to my digs knowing full well I wouldn't be able to sit there for long. It felt like every night was Sunday night and I hadn't done my homework. So, I'd mooch down to Shepherd's Bush and annoy the Bush staff into coming out for a drink. I had a right couple of hangovers that week. And I reckon that helped me stop worrying about the fact that my play was about a theatre critic who falls in love with an actress and ends up working for vampires. I was too tired to worry.

The next place we rehearsed was a church hall in White City. We were very cold. There was a large fan heater but it made so much noise we couldn't work with it on. It heated the air rather than the room. You could leave it on for two hours and as soon as you turned it off, you might as well have been outside. (No, it was warmer outside.)

By this time there were more of us in the room, our assistant director Helen and our stage manager Zoe. Things were a bit more chatty. Brian told us stories about working in famous classical productions and Hollywood movies. And we just sort of drank our tea.

Brian was working with an accent coach from Dublin. For a week or two he sounded like he'd lived in a caravan in every county in Ireland, especially when he got tired. But he worked his bollocks off and began to sound quite good as the production neared. He reminded me of an uncle I had in Dublin.

We spoke about the play. We liked the character. He was honest. We felt sorry for him. We were afraid the critics would attack us for portraying one of their number in such a degrading fashion. I was also afraid they'd knock me for not writing an ensemble play which many of them suggested I do after my first Bush production, *This Lime Tree Bower*. We veered from strutting arrogance to stumbling cowardice and back again.

We started doing interviews.

Brian came to Dublin. We walked around the places where I imagined the play happened. We did some shopping. Brian tried his accent out.

The next place we rehearsed was Latvia House. This was a cultural centre for Latvian expatriates near Hyde Park. I felt at home there. It might have been something to do with my Catholic upbringing. Latvia House was full of images: depictions of battles, portraits of dignitaries, emblems with birds on them. We were in a large first-storey room with a wooden floor and high windows, which opened onto a balcony where we could smoke.

There was a place nearby where we could get sandwiches and so on. Brian and I sat there one lunchtime and became intrigued with the waitress's accent. She was very beautiful, very dark, she sounded Eastern European. I told Brian she reminded me of what the vampires might be like in the play. Brian said, 'She's Russian.' He had done a lot of work in Russia and was a bit of a Russophile. He called her over. I was going, 'No, Brian, don't . . . '

Brian goes, 'Hi. Are you Russian?'

She goes, 'No. Not Russian,' and walks off without elaboration. Perhaps even a little insulted.

I said, 'Brian, that's quite a gift you've got there. You want to cultivate that.' Brian just laughed and began eyeing the cakes.

We finally moved to the Bush itself for a few rehearsals before previewing. We went into town and bought a costume. Brian wore it all the time. (He even got food on it one night before going on. An elderly man beside me in the audience asked me if the stains were deliberate. I said yes.)

Brian threw a party at his house. We were made to take our shoes off on arrival. At first I was annoyed, thinking this was some bullshit religious observance, until Brian told me to relax, it was just so we'd feel the benefit of his underfloor heating. There was a lot of champagne. A group of us ended up in the back garden, still in our bare feet in what must have been four or five degrees. Those of us not used to champagne invented a character who wants to impress everyone with his rubbish take on the finer things in life.

We left at about seven in the morning.

We opened. Press night had about twenty-five critics. I sat waiting for the moment when Brian says, 'Mmm. I was a bollocks to all the other critics. And I'll tell you why, because it was this: they were all cunts.' I could remember writing that line one afternoon when I was living with my girlfriend in Leicester. I could remember my mischievous self-satisfaction, thinking what a great fellow I was altogether. And now here it was ringing out over a roomful of critics. There was a silence like someone had pressed the detonator and nothing happened. And then bang, the place erupted. We were all playing.

Brian was fantastic.

I was terrified about how we were going to be received in the papers. Were we having a cheap jibe at an easy target, or were we exploring the nature of reason and responsibility? To tell you the truth I couldn't be sure any more. If the reviews were bad, I probably wanted the play to be me getting my digs in first. If they were good I wanted the play to induct me and Brian into a community that included artists, audiences *and* critics for however long it lasted. I was a picture of fickle self-preservation.

The morning the reviews came out I was on my way to a reading of my new play, *The Weir*, at the Royal Court. I bought the papers on the way. And I immediately knew we were alright. They knew they'd seen a brilliant piece of acting from Brian, and thankfully that spilled over to include the things he had been able to bring out in my writing. They were bigger men and women than most of us usually give them credit for. But we all suspect that from time to time, in our more self-confident moments perhaps.

I walked into the Royal Court every inch the young-playwright-about-town. More than a bit smug.

Towards the end of the run I went back to the Bush after a sobering few weeks in Dublin. Dominic Dromgoole, who had commissioned *St Nicholas* before going to work at the Old Vic, came to see the show with his partner Sasha and their new baby Grainne. Grainne was about four weeks old and too young to be left with a sitter. My girlfriend, Ríonach, offered to mind her in the dressing room during the show so Sasha could see it and still feed the baby at the interval.

I sat there for a while in the dark dressing room while Ríonach walked around with Grainne in her arms. She said, 'She keeps moving so she can hear my heart.' She slept there, across Ríonach's chest. Over the intercom we could hear Brian's performance and I wondered which was putting Grainne to sleep,

Ríonach's heartbeat or the dead weight of my writing. But I didn't really care. The child in Ríonach's arms. And me dripping in lousy perspective.

Conor McPherson
Dublin, February 1999